CASHING IN ON COOKING

CASHING IN ON COOKING

Nancy C. Baker

Contemporary Books, Inc.
Chicago

Library of Congress Cataloging in Publication Data

Baker, Nancy C.
   Cashing in on cooking.

   Includes index.
   1. Cookery.   2. Self-employed.   3. Small business.
I. Title.
TX652.B3125   1982   642'.068   81-69604
ISBN 0-8092-5873-0 (pbk.)   AACR2

Published by Contemporary Books, Inc.
180 North Michigan Avenue, Chicago, Illinois 60601
Manufactured in the United States of America
Library of Congress Catalog Card Number: 81-69604
International Standard Book Number: 0-8092-5873-0 (paper)

Published simultaneously in Canada by
Beaverbooks, Ltd.
150 Lesmill Road
Don Mills, Ontario M3B 2T5
Canada

To my parents, Billie and Don Moll

Contents

Introduction

Do you bake the best cherry cheesecake in town? Or is your specialty red hot chili con carne, fresh strawberry jam, or possibly, homemade banana bread? Do guests leave your parties raving about your cooking and your hospitality? If so, you may be one of the thousands of people who've dreamed about basing a career—from a part-time job to their very own small business—on their cooking skills.

In today's inflationary economy, every road to extra income is a welcome one, so many good cooks are turning their abilities with food into cash—from extra pocket money to a full fledged business income. They are taking advantage of our changing society—one where more and more women are working outside the home, thus having less time to spend cooking for their families. These working wives and mothers are much more likely to buy food services from others; this creates expanding opportunities for good cooks to profit from their cooking skills.

Such profit is possible for you, too, whether you've been bound to your home kitchen as a housewife (or househusband) or have worked for years at another kind of job and cooked only as a hobby. What it takes is a true love of cooking as well as certain other skills and personality factors.

The people profiled in this book have all made the change to careers in cooking. None has a degree in home economics or training at the Cordon Bleu, not because such credentials would be a detriment, but because they're out of reach for most people. They have homegrown and refined cooking skills of all kinds, from Helen Benton's ability to invent a low-calorie whipped topping that won't fall to Charles Baron's cooking and serving six-course French dinners for his very impressed friends.

The time commitments they've made to their work with food ranges from Marcia Matthews' 20 hours a week as a freelance pastry chef to Nadine Kalachnikoff's 14-hour days running her own take-out food store. They chose their careers working with foods for a variety of reasons, too, ranging from Sandy Gooch's passion for pure foods following her near death from an allergic reaction to something she'd eaten, to Tom Wagstaff's dream of running his own business. And their ages when they began their careers in cooking range from Judy Prindle's 15 to Charles Baron's "retirement age."

The kinds of businesses these cooking entrepreneurs chose run the gamut, too, from bakeries to restaurants, from freelance food styling to cooking and freezing convenience foods, from specialty food shops to teaching others to cook, from catering businesses to writing about cooking.

If you want to try your hand at cooking for cash, the experiences of these people can help you decide what kind of career is right for you. And they will help you avoid some of the pitfalls they ran across, too. You'll see that there are some special considerations for food businesses that don't apply to other kinds of enterprises—the perishability of your products, for example. And there are certain legal requirements that you'll need to know and understand as well. The government is pledged to protect the public health from contaminated food, and that means additional restrictions (some say headaches) for you if you plan to cook for public consumption.

Through this book, you'll learn what non-cooking skills and personality factors are important for success in your own small business or freelance cooking career. For example, you might be the world's best cook and yet be unsuited for the pressures of running your own restaurant. Or you might decide to take in a partner who has the business and financial skills you might lack.

The U.S. Labor Department says that the demand for cooks will increase faster than the average for all occupations at least through the mid-1980s. The opportunities are there; the keys are confidence and creativity. With this book as your guide, and with some effort, careful planning, and your ability as a good cook, soon you, too, can be cashing in on cooking.

1

Tap the Take-Out Business

Today, more than half of the women of working age are employed outside their homes. That means many changes for American society, not the least of which is that these women are no longer spending as many hours in their kitchens preparing their families' favorite meals.

The size of the typical American household is shrinking, too. More people live alone, couples have children later in life or not at all, elderly people who are often single live longer. Many of these smaller households don't like to go to the trouble of preparing special meals for only one or two. It's hard, after all, to justify cooking an entire turkey or a beef roast, or to spend hours preparing a baked Alaska for dessert, and then eat it alone. And the leftovers for a small household often last far longer than people want to eat them, or else they go to waste.

All this means that Americans today are likely to spend more money in the grocery store, much of it spent on convenience foods that require less preparation time at home, like frozen dinners. And they're likely, too, to stop on the way home from work and buy a prepared or partially prepared meal from a take-out store. That could mean something as simple as picking up a pizza from the local Shakey's or a tub of chicken from Colonel Sanders. Or it could mean that they're patronizing one of the proliferation of small businesses being started by good cooks who can provide them with truly special take-out food, the kind of food more people would prepare themselves if they had the time. These shops also offer the kinds of food whose preparation at home is really justified only when at least five or six will be at the dinner table.

Nadine Kalachnikoff of Washington, D.C., started such a business just as the 1980s dawned. Called Pasta, Inc., it's located in the city's Georgetown section and it sells complete dinners, from appetizers to luscious desserts, all to take out.

Separated from her husband in 1978, Nadine's incentive for going into business was a common one for many modern women: she had to find a way to support herself and her two young sons, then ages 1 and 4. She'd always been a wonderful cook, learning from childhood under the direction of her mother and grandmother. She had considered opening a restaurant, but thought that the time demands would take too much away from her duties as a mother. One summer night in 1979, she felt a passion for some *risotto* and thought, "Wouldn't it be great if there were a place where people could buy a complete meal, from first course through last, to take home?" And the idea for Pasta, Inc., was born.

Nadine, who was born in Paris, is of Spanish and Russian heritage. Interestingly, her store features largely Italian main courses and French desserts. She began building her dream by going to Milan to find just the right pasta machines. Pasta, Inc., features, among other specialties, homemade pasta and a variety of sauces. Customers simply boil the

pasta at home and heat the sauce they select and—voila!—
an Italian dinner worthy of an afternoon spent over a hot
stove.

After she conceived the idea for Pasta, Inc., and found a
Georgetown location she thought would be appropriate,
Nadine went to a bank to finance the project. "I brought
along the woman who owned my store space, offered my
house as collateral and borrowed $100,000," Nadine says.
The bank required her to supply a written proposal of her
idea and a projection of her income, which she did. Financing was no real problem, she says, "because my home is
worth more than $100,000. I didn't need a business loan and
this way there is less risk for the bank."

Nadine spent more than six months planning her business
before it opened, partly, she says, because "my older son,
Howard, was so affected by the divorce. I included him in
the plans for the store. I even took him down there while
we were remodeling and gave him a hammer so he could
help. At first, he didn't want me to have the business. He
wanted a toy store, if anything. But recently, someone asked
him what he wants to be when he grows up and he said,
'President of Pasta, Inc.'"

Nadine decorated her store basically in white: white walls,
a white tile floor, white ceiling fans. In the window are pasta
machines spewing forth four varieties of pasta: spinach,
tomato, egg, and whole wheat. Dried herbs and shiny
copper pots are hung over the counter, which displays salads
and cheeses for sale.

When the store opened in February, 1980, word spread
quickly and customers flocked in. In her first six weeks in
business, Nadine grossed $75,000. Getting things totally
organized and under control, however was not quite as easy
as was attracting customers.

"I didn't realize at first the amount of responsibility I was
taking on by opening this business," Nadine says. "There
was a time when I definitely felt I was in over my head. I
wasn't enjoying it and I was hardly ever seeing my children."
At first, Nadine often worked until 2:00 a.m. Even with a

kitchen staff of five, she tried to do everything herself. When she saw herself beginning to fold under the pressure, she sat down and reconsidered her commitment. "I saw that everyone else was taking home income from my shop and I wasn't. And I thought it wasn't going to be worth it if I wasn't enjoying what I was doing. I considered quitting. But I thought, 'No, this is what I want for my future and my children's.' I love cooking and I love doing all the jobs at Pasta, Inc. I decided I needed to delegate more responsibility. Now I have three people who can do many of the jobs and I am busy learning the bookkeeping."

Nadine began to realize what many new business owners in the food industry find—cooking is only one part of the business and she couldn't do everything herself. "I should have done things like the bookkeeping in the first place," she says, "but instead, I was making the mozzarella. It's a matter of priorities. The bookkeeping is much more important to the business. When you touch money, everything changes."

Even so, Nadine knows that she has to be able to do all the jobs at Pasta, Inc., in case someone else quits or makes unreasonable demands. "I can't afford to be in a position where the shop can't function if one person leaves." Recently, she had to fire an employee and that action meant she would have to do that job herself until a replacement was found. Back to the 14-hour days, at least temporarily.

While Nadine's foods have always earned her praise, she is a creative cook, not a recipe-follower, and she had never measured ingredients before opening her store. As a result of her cooking style, she found it very difficult to price her products. "I've learned to measure, but I still sometimes throw in a dash of something else in the end and there go the profits," she says. Her manager has helped her price her foods, largely by following her around, notebook in hand, while she cooks and noting the ingredients and amounts she uses.

"I'm embarrassed and shocked at the prices I have to charge," she says. "It's all that Swiss chocolate and butter."

A few of those prices in the store's early months: $2.69 a pound for pasta; from $2.85 to $6.50 for 14 ounces of sauce (including nutmeg, summer and winter tomato, pesto, and others; $5.75 a pound for lasagna; $5.95 a pound for ravioli.

Pasta, Inc., has many of the same expenses as a restaurant, except for the linens. Nadine points out, "I have the same kitchen, my sales people are the same as waiters." But she thinks her customers are getting a better bargain despite the somewhat high prices. "If you go to a restaurant, you aren't served a pound of lasagna. You get maybe a quarter pound. My portions serve more than one person."

When the store first opened, Nadine had a certain amount of waste and spoilage, but with time she learned how to judge what quantity of a perishable product was likely to be sold on a specific day and was able to plan accordingly. Everything except bread and wine is prepared in her kitchen.

Location for a store like Pasta, Inc., is always a key factor and Nadine chose wisely. The affluent Georgetown area was obviously looking for just such a shop and people there were willing and able to pay the prices she found necessary to charge.

Many of Washington's socialites have patronized Pasta, Inc., and Nadine has also enjoyed excellent media coverage and word-of-mouth advertising. One piece of publicity she's particularly proud of: "I was on Voice of America telling the Russians how I, a woman from an immigrant Russian family, have my own business. That was a real thrill for me."

She's also opened a catering sideline for the business and has among her customers the Charles Percys and Evangeline Bruce. And, in 1980, she was hired to bake the birthday cake for Miss Lillian Carter.

Ironically, the business that was started so Nadine Kalachnikoff could better support her children has tended to separate her from them. She's hired a young woman to live in and take care of her sons when they're not in school. "They take a nap when they come home from school and then I try to get home in the evening to spend an hour with them. After that, I usually have to come back to work. When the sitter is off, I bring the kids to the store with me and they play here." She points out, however, that her young sons are exceptionally well-behaved for their ages. "If they were running around the shop making noise, I couldn't stand it."

When the children are ill, "that's my priority," she says. "I just go home. My younger son, Chris, has a tendency toward tonsillitis and ear infections and, when he's ill, I simply have to be with him." Luckily, she now has three employees who can take over for her in such emergencies.

Nadine's goal is to be able to support herself and her sons from the profits of Pasta, Inc., by 1983. "Then, I want to be able to take them camping and journey down the Snake River or anything else we want to do."

In the meantime, she's found she can't really take a salary out of the store yet. All her profits are ploughed back into paying off that $100,000 loan and expanding the business, so she has to live on other income. One of her clever and successful expansion ideas is the "in-home pasta man" who goes to a customer's home and cooks there, preparing sauces in chafing dishes and serving freshly tossed pasta and salad to any number of guests. The pasta man and another cook are priced at $150 for an evening, plus the cost of the food. An idea like the "pasta man" does well in sociable, affluent Georgetown, but it probably wouldn't work nearly as well—at least not at that price—in a smaller city like Spokane or Oklahoma City.

Ideas for the expansion of Pasta, Inc., that will work in her town are not Nadine Kalachnikoff's problem. How to attract more business to the shop isn't either. He main problem is one most other small business owners would love to have: how to handle the amazing overnight success her project has already generated.

Peggy Mathison of Playa del Rey, California, had virtually the same idea as Nadine—that there should be a place where people can buy a complete quality dinner, from hors d'oeuvres to dessert, to take out. She implemented her idea by creating a line of frozen gourmet entrees, side dishes, and desserts, and with five other women opened Custom Cookery.

Custom Cookery hasn't yet experienced the success that Pasta, Inc., has, although Peggy hopes it will someday. The company has suffered from a combination of bureaucratic hassles, a rocky economy, and the women's lack of experience in the business world. Peggy agreed to tell her business' story to help others avoid the pitfalls she and her partners have encountered.

Peggy says she had thought about starting a company like Custom Cookery for 20 years while she worked in public relations, magazine editing, and college administration. In her leisure time, she was well known as an excellent cook. Then, in 1977, she left her job, deciding the time was right to act on her idea for a convenience foods business.

"There were so many people out working by then that I thought they'd like a place to buy a dinner like ours. Our market is working people who appreciate good food and who care about what they put into their bodies, but who don't have time to cook the kind of meals we sell. We use only the best ingredients, nothing artificial." Menu items include salmon mousse ($4.00), chicken Ann Marie ($4.25), beef *bourguignon* ($4.95) and more than a dozen others.

Peggy talked to friends about her idea and found they were enthusiastic about going into business with her. She invested her own money, totalling $65,000 over a four-year period, and took out a $40,000 bank loan guaranteed by the Small Business Administration. Her five partners invested much smaller amounts and became minor stockholders. By late 1978, they had rented space in a restaurant kitchen, as well as space that was to become a combination retail store and new kitchen of their own. They located in Playa del Rey, a small seaside community within the Los Angeles city limits. They tested their favorite recipes and found that some didn't freeze well and others didn't pass the group's taste test, but ultimately they chose a variety that pleased everyone. They hammered, nailed, cleaned, painted, and got the store space in shape, and Custom Cookery was in business. They hired professional builders to begin on their new kitchen.

The women of Custom Cookery worked a variable number of hours. Between the six of them, they had 23 children ranging in age from 10 to 33. Everyone but Peggy wanted part-time rather than full-time work. "We really supported each other," Peggy says. "If someone had a sick child, we'd work around her so she could be at home." The working atmosphere was one of camaraderie as the women built a business on their considerable combined cooking skills.

However, the store location they had chosen turned out to be a mistake. The pedestrian traffic near it is not sufficient to provide the kind of business Peggy had hoped for, and because it's near the beach, not many people drive by. Those who don't actually live in Playa del Rey seldom go there except to enjoy the seashore. And beach-goers proved not to be inclined to buy frozen foods and carry them home.

Building the new kitchen was even a bigger mistake, Peggy admits. "We got a quick okay of our plans from the health department, so that was no problem. But the building and safety department was something else." The women of Custom Cookery spent months trying to cut the red tape of that bureaucratic agency. "Every time we dealt with those people, they would demand something else be changed," Peggy says. One requirement was one parking space for every 500 square feet of space in the store. The building has an adjacent lot that they were using for parking. That lot, however, happens to be on city property. "Our landlord had rented it from the department of parks and recreation for 12 years," she says, "and he got a letter from that agency saying it had no intention of changing anything. But the building and safety people said that wasn't good enough. We had to *own* a parking lot."

Irate at the treatment she was receiving, Peggy contacted the deputy mayor of Los Angeles. After word of her plight was passed down the ranks, she was called to still another meeting with building and safety officials. "This time they told us that we'd built our kitchen in a space that should have been the garage for an apartment over our store. In other words, there was no way they were going to give us an okay to use that kitchen. They said our landlord could apply to the building and safety commission for a variance. He promised to do that, but he never did." By the time the kitchen was built and it was determined that Custom Cookery's chances of using it legally were almost nonexistent, they'd been in business well over a year and the national economy was hitting a definite downturn.

"In the summer of 1980," Peggy says, "business was getting very bad. It was bad for everyone, if they're honest about it. I knew we had a great product that people would buy if they only knew about it, but I needed to find a way to make more money. I thought we could keep the store for the retail trade, but I also hoped we could go wholesale— sell our products to health food stores and small specialized markets. That was *really* a mistake."

Things looked great at first. Peggy made a huge sale to a chain of 18 specialty food stores in southern California. "I prepared a sample kit of our foods and gave it to the store owner and he absolutely loved it. He said our food was wonderful. He ordered 3000 units of our most expensive item, scallops in tarragon cream."

Custom Cookery was not set up to supply that kind of quantity, however. The women had cooked only a dozen or so packages of a dish at a time, and they specialized in cooking in small quantities to insure flavor and quality. Peggy and her partners didn't want to pass up a sale like that, though, so they hired more cooks and got a special price on ingredients like scallops and cucumbers by buying in large quantities. They purchased packaging and special labels that carried the specialty store's name, not Custom Cookery's. And production got underway. "He wanted the 3000 units in two weeks," Peggy recalls. "I didn't think we could do it that fast, but actually we finished in just over two weeks." To make the deadline, their cooking techniques had to change. Until then, the women had sautéed their scallops by hand, for example. But, "with 3000 to prepare, we just couldn't do that anymore. We learned a lot about how to take shortcuts without affecting the quality of the food."

One thing they didn't learn in time, however, was how much it would actually cost them to produce the food and what wholesale prices to charge so they would still make a profit. Custom Cookery had been selling its scallops in tarragon cream to retail customers for $5.25 a serving. They sold that same size to the specialty food store for $2.60 a serving. It wasn't enough. "When you're cooking in small quantities," Peggy says, "you don't worry about the cost of something like tarragon. You don't use that much. But suddenly here we were, buying tarragon by the pound, and it costs $17.50 a pound. That really affects your profit margin. We ended up having to rent frozen-food lockers, too, to store the products until the store took delivery. I hadn't planned for that, either. I had to hire more people to cook, so that increased our workmen's compensation costs. And we had to increase our liability insurance, so that cost more, too."

As soon as Custom Cookery had delivered its first batch of 3000 scallop entrees, the specialty store ordered another 3000. "Then I really got nervous," Peggy says. "I didn't see how they could sell that many, but the owner reassured me. He said that this was just the beginning. He said he would be ordering other things from our menu, too, and he was sure we'd be very successful together. So I was lulled into thinking we were going to make it big." They started cooking all over again, and because they were so busy filling the wholesale orders, they closed the ailing retail section.

When the second large order had been filled, Peggy approached other markets and got more orders. These turned out to be even more trouble, however. "Most of the other stores asked that we come in and give demonstrations. That cost us money for the food and for the demonstrator's time." Peggy by this time had learned to adjust her prices upward so that they would make a profit. But now they found another truth of hard economic times: the small businessman is usually the last to be paid.

"Most of these stores *still* haven't paid us," she said, and it's been months now. We don't have that kind of cushion. I have to pay my suppliers. I have to pay my employees. I have to pay my rent and insurance and make payments on my loan. If I'm not paid by my customers, I'm not in business."

Although her first wholesale customer paid on time, Peggy says, "I was right. He couldn't sell all those units of scallops. A friend of mine was in one of his stores last week and she says he still has some in the freezer case. Needless to say, the thousands of orders of our other products that we'd expected never materialized. We never heard from him again."

So, in the spring of 1981, Peggy Mathison and her partners in Custom Cookery decided to regroup. One woman decided to get out of the business altogether and the others decided to cut their losses with the Playa del Rey store and its doomed kitchen, and with wholesaling. They put their kitchen equipment in storage, happy to be finished dealing with the building and safety people and with their uncooperative landlord. And they decided to do what Peggy now thinks they should have done a year earlier. "We should have moved the retail store to another neighborhood and rented, not built, a commercial kitchen somewhere else. We're planning to do that now."

Peggy is working with a young college business major who will earn academic credit for doing a feasibility study for her. He will study half a dozen neighborhood business areas to determine where Custom Cookery should open its new store. He will analyze such factors as pedestrian traffic, affluence of the people who live and work nearby, rents in the area, and the local competition in convenience foods. Custom Cookery undoubtedly would have benefitted from such a study before the decision to open in Playa del Rey was made.

"I no longer think the kitchen and the retail outlet should

be in the same place," Peggy says. "We can make do with 500 square feet of space for a retail store. I want it small and elegant. We can rent a kitchen in a commercial district. There's no need to pay high rent to have the kitchen in an affluent neighborhood." She says she'll rent an already licensed kitchen this time. No more headaches with bureaucracy for her. "I know a caterer and we may share his kitchen. We can cook four days a week, or maybe five half days. With frozen food we don't have to worry about having things fresh every day."

Custom Cookery will include more fresh foods on the menu this time around—mainly pâtés, soups, homemade mayonnaise and salad dressings. But even those will have a shelf life of three or four days, Peggy says. A big advantage of the frozen entrées, side dishes, and desserts, of course, is that "we don't waste anything. Our foods would probably stay fresh for months in the freezer, although we've put a limit of six weeks on how long we'll keep them." Custom Cookery is never faced with an extra pot of something that will spoil if it's not sold today.

Peggy Mathison is convinced that Custom Cookery is still an excellent idea for a convenience foods business. And she's also sure that the time is right for it. More people are working outside the home. The 1980 census shows that the average number of people living in each household is now down to only 2.75. People, particularly in southern California, are becoming more and more aware of what's actually in the foods they eat. ("Have you looked at some of the labels in the frozen foods department of the supermarket?" she asks. "Some of those things hardly contain any *food*. They're all additives and chemicals.")

Eventually, Peggy would like to see retail outlets for Custom Cookery in many of the more affluent areas of southern California. The cooking could still be done at one central kitchen and she thinks the retail outlets would be excellent investments for other women who want their own small businesses. In order to achieve that goal, however, she and her partners will have to establish their business successfully in one carefully selected location. And they will need to obtain more capital to finance such an expansion, too. In the spring of 1981, that didn't look too easy to do. "Two years ago," Peggy said, "I borrowed $40,000 at 12 percent interest. I should have borrowed 7240,000. Now I'd have to pay 22 percent for the same loan."

Custom Cookery has been the victim of a lot of bad luck and some business mistakes, Peggy Mathison feels. But she's determined to learn from experience and make the second time around the successful time around for her convenience foods business.

Have you an idea for your own convenience foods business? If so, take some pointers from Nadine Kalachnikoff's success and Peggy Mathison's initial frustrations.

Surely, a strong market for quality convenience foods exists today. The upsurge in sales of quickly prepared foods sold in supermarkets supports that theory. If people will buy macaroni-and-cheese mixes and frozen pizzas to save time in the kitchen, it makes sense that they'll also buy a higher quality item like Custom Cookery's shepherd's pie or Pasta, Inc.'s Corfu salad, which are also ready in minutes.

As Peggy Mathison's experience details, however, it's not as simple as just having an idea and opening a store. There are several major things you must consider and plan for first.

The most important is your product. What's different about it? What makes it better than foods your potential customers could buy on their weekly shopping trips to a market? Remember, your customers want to buy convenience foods to save time. Yet, it costs them time to patronize your store. Your product is more than wonderful food; it's also the convenience of time saved for activities other than cooking.

Your best course of action may well be to begin with a variety of food items, doing a careful market study of each with an eye to expanding production of those that sell well and eliminating those that don't. Peggy says, "We were really surprised to see some of our foods that sold well and some that didn't. For instance, we all loved our pork chops with savory beans done in wine and herbs, but the customers just didn't buy them. So we discontinued that item. On the other hand, we had sudden runs on some things so that we could hardly keep up with production. At one time our most popular item was enchiladas with green sauce. Don't ask me why."

When you consider your product, you must also look at your fast-food chain competitors. If you want to sell take-out chicken, for example, it will have to be much different than that offered by Kentucky Fried Chicken. Because of the large quantity of food such chains sell, they can set their prices well below what you would have to charge and still make a handsome profit. Will people pay more for your chicken? Why?

If you're convinced that you can sell just one item in your convenience food store, remember that you'll have to sell to more customers. If you offer only spaghetti, for example, how often will repeat customers patronize your store? Once a week? Once every two weeks? Less often? If you offer a variety of items, you may see the same customer two or three times a week. Or, if you offer frozen entrees like Custom Cookery, you might sell half a dozen to a customer at a time. He could take them home, put them in his freezer, and pop them into his oven on nights when he's not inclined to do much cooking.

The pricing of convenience foods can be just as difficult as pricing a restaurant menu, and both Nadine Kalachnikoff and Peggy Mathison had problems with this area of business management. You must be able to compute *exactly* how much each of your ingredients costs you, including such small quantity items as spices. Remember, as Peggy Mathison found out the hard way, that a pinch of tarragon adds up when you're producing large quantities. And that can be just the thing that overloads your expenses and eats up your profit if you haven't planned for it.

If your business, like Nadine's, involves fresh foods, remember to figure in waste. A pot of spaghetti sauce or bowl of salad greens can't be kept too long. And the foods that end up in the garbage will still cost you money.

Other important budget items are labor, both your own and any you hire; packaging; and such overhead items as store and kitchen-space rentals, insurance, and utility bills.

When you've calculated what you would have to charge for your convenience foods to make a fair profit, ask yourself (and those knowledgeable in the field) whether or not customers would actually pay your price. Chances are that, because your business will be small, your prices are going to be higher than what consumers would pay for a frozen dinner from the supermarket or a Big Mac and fries from the local McDonald's. So, not only will you have to offer something more unusual and of higher quality than the markets and fast food chains, you'll have to sell it to people who are willing and able to pay somewhat higher prices. You'll have to attract fairly affluent customers, and doing that depends a lot on both what you offer and where you offer it.

When you choose a retail outlet for your convenience foods business, it's well to take heed from the old cliché: there are three important things to consider when it comes to selecting real estate—location, location, and location. Nadine chose hers very well. She needed an affluent neighborhood with nearby pedestrian traffic and that's what she got in Georgetown. However, Peggy's choice in Playa del Rey, she admits, was not a good one; it led to many problems for Custom Cookery.

Before you sign a lease on a store, it's a good idea to have a feasibility study done, like the one Peggy Mathison has commissioned. Check such important details as the nearby foot traffic; the economic level of the people living nearby; the population density of the area; the local competition in quality, convenience, and fast food products; and the rent you'll have to pay.

Whether or not you'll need a kitchen attached to your retail outlet depends greatly on the kind of food you plan to sell. If it's a frozen food product, like that of Custom

Cookery, you may well benefit financially from separating your kitchen and retail outlet. Or, as Peggy plans for the future, you could have one central kitchen and several small retail outlets located in more expensive neighborhoods. To save money, at least until your new business gets on its feet, try to rent kitchen space. It's likely to be available in a restaurant that's open limited hours or from a caterer or baker.

If you plan to serve hot, freshly prepared foods, you'll need to have a kitchen adjacent to your sales space. Unless you can find such a building for lease (possibly a defunct bakery or small restaurant), you may have to rent a store and build your own kitchen. *Before* you sign the lease, check with the health department and other government agencies that may have jurisdiction over your kitchen. Building a new kitchen is expensive. Custom Cookery paid about $7000 for its ill-fated kitchen in 1978–79 and Peggy estimates a similar one today, with all new equipment, would cost upwards of $20,000. You don't want to be stuck with a lease on property where you can't build a kitchen that can be licensed. And, even more, you don't want to make Custom Cookery's error and spend money on a kitchen you ultimately can't use. Of course, if you decide to build a kitchen, there's no reason why all your equipment has to be brand new. Consider buying used equipment; if you buy wisely, you can save a tremendous amount of money that can be used elsewhere in your business.

You may be tempted to branch out and sell your products wholesale in addition to retail, but again, learn from Custom Cookery. There are several reasons why that company's products couldn't compete well in supermarkets against those produced by such national competitors as Stouffer's, and none of them has anything to do with quality.

One is price. Custom Cookery's foods were simply too high-priced for the supermarket trade. "One food store's biggest frozen food seller is macaroni and cheese," says Peggy. That just doesn't reflect the kind of sophisticated buyer who would pay $4.00 to $5.00 for a gourmet entrée.

A second reason is public recognition. "Stouffer's buys full-color ads in national magazines," Peggy points out, "so people recognize their name. We can't possibly afford to do that, so we're put in the position of having to give store demonstrations to get people to buy our products." Such demonstrations add to the costs of production and marketing and probably don't increase sales enough to warrant them.

A third reason is big business' attitude toward paying its small business suppliers in a time of high interest rates. Many small businesses are accustomed to waiting 90 days or longer for payment. Those who can't wait are going under. Even government is a culprit when it comes to paying small businesses on time. A recent study by the General Accounting Office, for example, showed that federal agencies had delayed paying 39 percent of their invoices beyond 30 days. Some remained unpaid for as long as seven months. And, of those paid late, 90 percent of the invoices were from small businesses. The reason, of course, is that in an unstable economy, it's financially wise to hold onto your money as long as possible before paying bills. And the small businessman has little clout with which to insist on payment. If Custom Cookery had declined to supply more frozen food products to its late-paying customers, for instance, the markets would have felt little pain. But if Stouffer's or Swanson did the same thing, undoubtedly the bill would be paid immediately. As a result, bills from large, important suppliers are paid first and the rest wait.

With a retail business, however, you won't have that problem. Your customers will pay you in cash when they receive your product, giving you the money to pay your bills promptly.

So, beware of expansion schemes that sound lucrative, until you've really checked them out carefully with sound business advice.

As with any new business, publicity is vital. If potential customers don't know you're there, they're not going to buy your product no matter how wonderful it is. Nadine Kalachnikoff's business benefitted from newspaper articles about it that appeared as far away as New York City. And, once people began patronizing her establishment, they liked what they found there, and their recommendations quickly brought in more business. So do whatever you can to draw attention to your new enterprise, whether it's holding a big grand opening ceremony or taking out paid ads in the local newspaper. Well-timed and favorable publicity is always time and money well spent and should be included in your company's budget.

With more and more people working outside their homes and American households shrinking in size, the market for quality convenience foods is there. If you have a viable idea, the right kind of customers waiting to patronize your company, access to the investment capital necessary for such a business, and the energy to start and run your own food enterprise . . . consider convenience foods.

2

Baking for Bread

Have you always dreamed of having your own bakery? Lots of good cooks, it seems, feel their specialties fall within the baked goods range, whether they excel with cheesecake, a bread specialty, cookies, muffins, or beautifully decorated cakes. After all, who can resist the aroma of fresh-baked bread? Or the tantilizing smell of chocolate chip cookies emerging from the oven?

There was a time when every neighborhood had its own bakery, just as every neighborhood had its own meat market and produce store. People shopped every day or two for bread and whatever other baked goodies caught their eye. But that day has passed. Now many bakeries are struggling to stay alive while supermarkets offer competition with a variety of breads and often a special bakery section as well.

So is there no place for a new bakery today? Some successful bakers think there is, but they insist on one important prerequisite: a truly unusual product. The day of the full-service neighborhood bakery may be over, but the day of the specialty bakery, for whose products people will drive miles and pay top dollar, is just dawning.

Loretta Shine has just such a bakery based in Beverly Hills and Encino, California—the Miss Grace Lemon Cake Company. Miss Grace began with just one product, a marvelous Bundt-shaped lemon cake, along with Loretta Shine's talent in the kitchen.

"I started in the food business by helping my sister-in-law make chocolate mousse pies in her kitchen to sell to restaurants," recalls Loretta. "It was her business, but when she wanted to go out of town, I'd take over for her. I discovered I liked meeting the chefs, and I liked getting out of the house."

Many women can understand Loretta's interest in the business. At that time, she had four children ranging in age from five to 14 and she was feeling house-bound. The business with her sister-in-law allowed her to have an interesting sideline, make some money, and yet be available to her children most of the time. It seemed almost too good to be true. Unfortunately, it was.

"The health department closed us down," Loretta recalls. "It's against California law to run a food concern out of your home kitchen (without modifying it to comply with acceptable health department standards), and it's almost impossible to make a home kitchen meet those standards, so we were through." So Loretta went back to being a housewife. But, by this time, she'd been bitten by the business bug. She still wanted to have that feeling of accomplishment that earning money through her own skills gave her. And her major skills at the time were those she had honed in her home kitchen.

"Shortly after we closed down, I was sitting at the Hollywood Bowl with a friend who mentioned that his aunt was selling the Miss Grace Lemon Cake Company, a small bakery in Beverly Hills that had just one product and a mailing list of 3000 names. It was just barely eking out an existence. I bought a dream and that's about all it was."

The terms of the purchase included a down payment and monthly payments over five years. Loretta's husband, Jack, served in an advisory capacity. "He's a builder and we combined his business knowledge with my cooking knowledge," she says. She was fortunate enough to be able to make the payments on the Miss Grace Lemon Cake Company from her profits over the five-year period.

Why was the company a success after Loretta bought it while it had been merely limping along under its previous owner? She thinks one reason is timing. "People were getting tired of junk food that was mass-produced. A quality item, like our lemon cake, was something they'd pay extra for." The cake is made from ingredients like fresh California lemons, butter, and eggs, and it's topped by a lemon glaze. It contains no preservatives or artificial flavorings. In 1980, the cakes sold for $9.25 each.

Loretta was also very fortunate to get some valuable free publicity shortly after she bought the place in the fall of 1973. "KNBC-TV was doing a series on unusual businesses and they gave us two minutes on the five o'clock news. They thought we were unusual because we had only one product. That was the first week in December and suddenly we were so busy that people had to have reservations to buy one of our cakes. We couldn't keep up with the demand. People would order two cakes and then beg me to sell them a third. One day we got so far behind that we just locked the door and put up a sign that said the oven was broken, come back in two hours, and they did. I was amazed."

Loretta's situation illustrates the value of publicity, something many food businesses learn when they receive their first big reviews. Good publicity sends people flocking in where there was little or no business the week before. She also learned quickly that she'd bought the Miss Grace Lemon Cake Company just as its busiest season of the year was beginning. "We've always done half our business between October and December," she says.

That first Christmas was never to be forgotten; it was a true trial by fire. Not only was the company overrun by customers lured by the television publicity, but the lemon cake became a major gift item. Today, Loretta says, "companies give us a list of maybe 200 names and we mail out cakes with their greetings."

During that first holiday season, Loretta's two older children, Robin, then 16, and Joel, then 13, earned money helping out in the store. When they tired, "we brought in sleeping bags and they slept on the counters while we worked all night," she remembers. At first, the business, like most new enterprises, was quite disruptive to the Shines' family life. "I thought I'd just hire a schoolgirl to sit for my younger children (Susan, then 9, and Danny, then 7), but I never seemed to get out until at least 6:00 p.m. and then there was heavy traffic until 7:00. Every night I was late."

Over the years, however, Loretta has found a balance between work and family life. One helpful recognition was that Christmas is *always* going to be terribly hectic. "Now we all know what Christmas is like and we expect it. We have to rent two additional spaces at that time, one to process the orders and one to ship out of. I tried doing it at home, but it disturbed everyone and just didn't work."

The frenzy of the busy season is tempered, however, by Loretta's attitude about her business. "I'm in a fortunate position because my husband supports us very well. What I do here won't affect the way we live terribly much. The one thing we do more of is travel and take nicer trips with the kids. That's partly because I felt so guilty about being away from the children while I was working."

The family's first trip was to Hawaii, and taking off like that while owning a new business is probably something no good business advisor would condone. Loretta felt her priorities should be with her family, however. "I just decided that, if the business couldn't get along without me for a week, I'd sell it." But it's been able to get along without her long enough to allow vacations with the family ever since. The Miss Grace Lemon Cake Company closes down for a week each year to allow all the employees to take a week off at the same time. Loretta couples that with a second week off during which her staff covers for her.

Another reason for Loretta Shine's success is that she and her husband took a hard look at the previous owner's sales techniques and decided they could use overhauling. For example, the original store sold to Saks and I. Magnin's "for the prestige," Loretta says. "When I bought it, I realized that I'd have to sell to those stores at a loss to keep their business. I'd say to Jack, 'How can I not sell to Saks?' and he'd say, 'How can you sell to them? You're in business to make money, not prestige.' So I lost all the accounts. I thought they were too important to lose at first, but Jack was convinced it was the right thing to do." She also learned the value of publicity from that early TV news spot. Now she courts it by such actions as donating cakes to celebrity charity events. "It gets the product tasted as well as the publicity," she says.

She's also added a handful of additional products to the roster of the Miss Grace Lemon Cake Company so that the product list now includes carrot cake, chocolate fudge cake, banana-pecan cake, and chocolate chip cookies in addition to the lemon cake. All the cakes are Bundt-shaped and covered with a glaze. 1980 prices ranged from $9.25 for the lemon cake and chocolate chip cookies to $12.00 for the chocolate fudge cake. Shipping adds $2.00 to the price within California and $3.50 outside California. Corporate customers who order more than 50 cakes receive a discount.

"Coming up with new products is tough," Loretta says. Her knowledge of foods was that of any good cook, not that of a trained home economist or nutrition expert, so trial-and-error prevailed. "I had zero knowledge. I read recipes and tried to combine them. With the chocolate fudge cake, for example, there was no recipe close to what I wanted. My cakes have to be shippable, which means firm and moist. They have to last without preservatives, because we don't use them. And, they have to be simple to make. That's no small list of requirements." After a multitude of false starts, however, Loretta found the right combination of ingredients for an almost sinfully delicious chocolate fudge cake. And then she repeated her process for the other items she's added to the menu.

When the business outgrew the Beverly Hills store, she turned that location into a retail outlet only and moved the kitchen to a location in Encino. Now all the baking is done in a second and newer location down the street from the first Encino spot because that one, also, became too small. The Miss Grace Lemon Cake Company now employs three bakers: Loretta's best friend, who runs a new division that will specialize in mousse; a full-time sales person; and Loretta's mother and mother-in-law, who rotate as sales persons in the Beverly Hills store. Temporary help are hired during the busy season as they're needed. Loretta has broken all the rules about not hiring friends and relatives, but it's worked out beautifully for her.

In eight years, Loretta Shine has grown from a housewife with an occasional sideline baking chocolate mousse pies to a true entrepreneur shipping cakes across the country. Her cakes have been featured in the *Washington Post, Town and Country, Women's Wear Daily, Seventeen,* and *Working Mother.* And she feels differently about herself now, too. "I like me much better now. I never knew I could do anything. I've learned about business and I would know what to do to make more money if my husband died and I had to support us. It requires a great deal of work, investment, and guts." She also thinks that her children have gained a different perspective on her. "It's been nice that they could work with me and I think they've gained respect for what I do and who I am."

When the business hits peaks, it's usual for Loretta's kids and husband to join the crew. "Once all my bakers wanted Good Friday off and we hadn't planned for it," she recalls, "so my older son came in and baked all the products." Her husband, Jack, is "my number one sampler and he helps with the bookwork and financial work when I go a little nutsy."

One of the advantages of having your own business when you're a working mother, Loretta Shine says, is that ability to take time off when family matters prevail, even it it's only for a PTA meeting. "I really like the freedom of being my own boss," she says.

And, with a product line as special as the cakes baked by the Miss Grace Lemon Cake Company, she has that freedom and a great deal of financial and personal success as well.

Loretta Shine saw a product that the public would pay for and she stepped in to provide it. That's the secret of any successful business, of course. It's not always easy to determine what kind of product the public needs and wants. And some that hit big turn out to be only fads. How long will the current craze of topping French croissants with everything from sliced ham to chocolate endure, for instance?

Another California baker, Helen Benton of Los Angeles, was certain her baked products would fill a public need. In 1973, Helen had tired of her catering business and sold it to relax at home. The only problem was that she found retirement boring. "About six or eight weeks after we got out of the catering business, I became bored and I was trying to think of what I could do. I think you can always go back and figure out what the needs of people are and then you've got a business," Helen says. When she worked as a caterer, she remembered constantly being asked questions like, "Does this have salt in it?" "Do you have anything low-calorie?" "Grandma's a diabetic; what can you offer for her?" "Do you know what kind of oil is used in this?" when she catered parties. "Also, my little niece is a diabetic," Helen says, "and I've watched my sister send her to birthday parties with her own little package of lunch that she could eat while the other children had ice cream and cake."

Helen also had friends who were involved with Weight Watchers franchises and she was interested in that program and its concept of food exchanges. "So, putting together all those things, I thought I'd just start a business that offered products without sugar and salt, and see what I could do with it."

That sounds a little easier than it was, however. There were no recipes for the kind of foods Helen had in mind. And often items baked with artificial sweeteners have a gagging aftertaste. She wanted her baked goods to taste as much like the fattening, sugar-and-salt-laden originals as possible. Achieving this end called for a great deal of experimentation.

Helen wanted to start with pies. She believed that you couldn't have a good pie without a dollop of whipped cream on it. "I remember being determined enough that I stayed in my own little kitchen for 28 hours straight trying to come up with a whipped cream that was low in calories and would stay whipped," she says. "I wanted to make the whipped cream without sugar and without a lot of butterfat in it, so obviously I had to start with nonfat milk. I could get it to stand up for awhile, but then it would collapse." After many more hours of experimentation in her kitchen, Helen finally was successful in creating a low-calorie whipped topping that stayed whipped.

Buoyed up by her success, she and her family decided to start a family business named The Thinnery. "We never really considered any other names," she says. "The Thinnery just seemed right. I guess we'd called regular bakeries 'fatteries.'" And the business has been charmed from the start. The Bentons leased a 1000-square-foot store in North Hollywood and Helen's husband, Bill, who had previously worked in the building industry, oversaw its conversion into a bakery.

"We got a second-hand showcase and a couple of refrigerators and baked in the back of the store," Helen recalls. "At first we offered just a few pies and it grew from there." At the time of this interview, The Thinnery featured more than 100 different products, and had a total of 34 stores in three states, several of which are distributorships that the Bentons have sold.

The Bentons were fortunate not to have to go to banks for financing in the beginning. "At first, we didn't really have that much of an investment—maybe $10,000 or $12,000 at the most. We generated our own income from the beginning. Business was that good because we found a need and filled it." On their first Mother's Day, for example, they sold $1000 worth of pies. "Before we went to the bank for money," Helen says, "we had nine stores and the bank actually came to us."

After only six months in business, Helen's experiments in the kitchen had greatly expanded the offerings of The Thinnery and the Bentons opened a second store in Woodland Hills. She also took in two partners, her friends with the Weight Watchers franchises. "Of course, they couldn't recommend our products under the Weight Watchers rules, but people knowing they were involved with us did help us get started."

The Thinnery's products average about 60 percent fewer calories than conventional baked goods and their labels list all ingredients as well as calories and food exchanges. Fruit is an important ingredient and is used for most of the sweetening in these items, often in quite an unexpected way. The Thinnery's chocolate cake, for example, is sweetened with bananas. The banana taste is not readily identifiable, though, and you'd think you were eating a typical chocolate cake with 60 percent more calories. The carrot cake is topped with a frosting made from ricotta cheese and a measured slice can replace a balanced meal because it contains vegetable, fruit, and protein from the cheese and dairy products.

Some artificial sweetener is used where sweet fruits like bananas and pineapple cannot provide the right flavor. Helen found that the Sweet'N'Low brand worked best for her ("It has some saccharin," she says, "but it's mostly lactose.") They use only 5 pounds of saccharin in 150,000 products, Helen says, although the law permits 30 mg. per serving.

The Thinnery's line of products has now expanded to include low-calorie salad dressings, ice milk, and specialties such as quiche, chili, and canneloni in addition to bakery products.

"I did all the original recipes, but my family helped me, too," Helen says. Unlike Loretta Shine's family, Helen Benton's has tended to stay with the business. Her daughter, Patti, was graduated from medical assistant training and got a job working for a doctor, but quit and rejoined her family's business when she discovered she didn't like blood all that much. Today, she's retail store supervisor for 14 stores. Bill Benton handles most of the business aspects, including pricing the products. And their two sons are now living in Washington, eagerly awaiting the expansion of The Thinnery chain into that state.

After two years in business, a new, much larger kitchen for The Thinnery was opened in Pacoima and today that facility does all the food preparation for 34 The Thinnery stores. It also contains a test kitchen where Helen concocts new products.

Because of the nature of their business, Helen says, they've had "a lot of interference from government agencies. Once we started shipping products out of our kitchen, we needed to have certain labels and certified laboratory analysis of everything. We got into a good deal of expense at that point. We have to substantiate our low-calorie claim. I think there are a lot of people claiming the same things we are who are getting away with unsubstantiated claims because they have only one or two stores. When we really began to grow, though, there were so many questions that I had the feeling that (the government agencies) were making up the rules for us." Helen's frustration echoes that of many in the food business who find it difficult and confusing to deal with government bureaucracy.

In the case of The Thinnery, the Bentons decided to try to keep one step ahead of the government, both to save future trouble and to serve their customers better. "We like to keep our labels up-to-date and maybe a year ahead of what the government agencies are going to ask for," Helen says. "We hired a woman who was very knowledgeable in labeling and she delved into every ingredient in all our products. Now we have complete files on everything we sell."

On the surface, it would seem that such a project could be done once and never need be repeated. However, The Thinnery buys some products that are prepared elsewhere and then uses them in their own items—for example, tomato sauce and pineapple chunks packed in their own juice. If the tomato sauce manufacturer, for instance, adds or subtracts something in his product, The Thinnery's labeling has to be changed. Helen has an agreement with all her suppliers that they won't change their products without notifying her, but that notification still will not save her from a certain amount of trouble and expense when such alterations occur.

Growth and shipping products from a central kitchen also changed the appearance of the Benton's foods. Now all items have to be packaged for shipment, sometimes more than 1000 miles away. Helen says, "A lot of our products lost their attractiveness. You couldn't just put something out on a shelf as a bakery item and sell it. Things are in boxes now—a beautiful cake looks great when you take it out of a box, but in the store, its beauty is hidden."

As the company grew, too, Helen began to take courses in food science. One such class, at California State University, Northridge, gave her information about the shelf life of food products and "the instructor showed slides of how food deteriorates over time." Helen, who had, until then, been proud to say that The Thinnery products contained no preservatives, was appalled. She immediately began studying what preservatives could be used and "the preservatives I do use now I try to have be derivatives of natural products such as seaweed." Their products are also kept refrigerated during shipment—an added cost, but necessary to their preservation.

The company doesn't plan to stop its expansion now. In 1981, Helen was in the process of selling several of the company-owned stores, but also was strongly considering opening another kitchen somewhere in the Midwest and another in northern California or Washington. The Midwest location became a possibility after an independent distributor there was able to sell a large quantity of The Thinnery products even though shipping them under refrigeration from southern California tripled their price.

"In five years, I think we'll be a national company," says Helen Benton. "I see continuous growth." Much of that growth will be possible because the Bentons, like all successful small-business owners, have lived quite frugally, putting most of the business' profits back into it, today creating a business grossing more than $2.5 million a year. "You have to be dedicated to your goals," she advises others. "You don't live high. It's a sacrifice."

Helen believes that the definition of success is "when you enjoy what you're doing, and I love it," so she sees herself as successful. She's worked long, hard hours over the past eight years with The Thinnery, but they've been enjoyable hours as well because Helen's always loved cooking and baking. And she's always loved having a business based on her interests and talents. And, of course, her business is also a success because she did what all the primers on starting a business advise—she found a public need and filled it.

If having your own bakery—like the Miss Grace Lemon Cake Company or The Thinnery, or your own personal vision—appeals to you, there are a few things to consider before signing a lease on a building, or deciding that your town will be wild for your apple kuchen.

The first, as we've said, is to make sure you have a product that's both unusual and desirable. That doesn't mean obscure, of course. There are plenty of unusual baked goods upon which it's doubtful that a successful business could be built. Some do not have enough devotees to comprise even a small list of customers, others are too perishable or too expensive, or complicated to produce. And still others are tied to growing seasons (like fresh raspberry pies, for example). Your product needs to be one that has a number of fans, is easy to bake, has a reasonable shelf life, and isn't overly expensive to bake.

Watch out, too, for faddish products. Stick to the kind of baked goods that have stood the test of time. For instance, you might be able to build a bakery business on providing brownies and other kinds of bar cookies. We all remember them from our childhoods and our parents probably do from theirs as well. Famous Amos, after all, built a small empire on the chocolate chip cookie.

Be sure, too, that you are judging your baked items without bias. Just because you, your children, and your Aunt Sarah are crazy about your caramel rolls doesn't mean that everyone will be. Take a hint from Loretta Shine and donate your specialty in return for the reactions of some non-paying customers. Well before you commit yourself to going into business, bake a quantity and supply a local school carnival or club fundraiser. Request an honest appraisal of your product's appeal and ask your tasters how much they'd be willing to pay for your baked item, were it for sale locally.

Make certain, as well, that your specialty is not one that would have to compete with a national chain of stores that could produce something similar at a lower cost. For example, your doughnut shop would have to be pretty special to steal business from the Winchell's down the street.

Does the baked product you have in mind lend itself to shipping? If it could become a successful gift item, your business, like the Miss Grace Lemon Cake Company, could attract national customers. One advantage of mail-order sales is being able to plan ahead—the orders are in hand before you open one sack of flour or crack your first eggshell. This greatly reduces your waste. And often you can collect at least some of your money prior to baking your product. What this means, however, is that your baked good has to be the kind of item that a company would be proud to offer as an image-enhancing gift. It also means your product must have a particularly long shelf life. Sourdough bread baked in San Francisco that's hard as a rock by the time it arrives in Maine, for instance, would hardly be a good choice.

Remember, too, the requirements of packaging and labeling if you're thinking of packing and shipping your products. Loretta Shine ships her cakes in round metal boxes (the kind many people like to save because they're so great for keeping fruitcakes and Christmas cookies fresh during the holidays). And The Thinnery's products are packaged in a variety of ways. A small carrot cake is offered in an aluminum pan covered by a plastic dome. Decorated cakes are placed in traditional bakery boxes. Spice bars are packaged on a plastic tray and covered with cellophane.

If you're dependent on the U.S. mail or a private shipping

service for delivery, as is the Miss Grace Lemon Cake Company, you'll need *very* sturdy wrapping to assure that your products will get to their destinations. If like The Thinnery, however, you'll be transporting your products in your own trucks to retail outlets only, you can get by with a lighter wrapping and a smaller expenditure for packaging.

Carefully consider how much it will cost you to produce your baked items; add in your labor, sales costs, shipping, insurance, packaging, store rent, etc., and compute how much you'd have to charge for them to make a reasonable profit. Loretta Shine points out that labor and the cost of ingredients will probably be at least 50 percent of the cost of the finished product. Is the figure you compute competitive? Will people pay that much for your specialty?

For something like her cakes, Loretta advises, "Don't worry about having an expensive product. People will pay the price if you're offering top quality." That may not be true for all kinds of baked goods, however.

Helen Benton notices that people are often fairly frugal when they visit The Thinnery stores. "I think it's psychological," she says. Many people who patronize a place like The Thinnery are trying to lose weight, so they're very conscious of what they're doing there. They may feel a little sinful for buying that fruit danish even if its calories are significantly fewer than the supermarket's variety. So they buy more carefully, Helen says. "Many people know that if they buy one more than they need, they're likely to go home and eat it, so they're careful about quantity. They might go into another bakery and spend $9.00, but if they go into one of our stores and spend $9.00, we hear about it." So, partly as a result of recognizing this psychology, the Bentons make every effort to keep their low-calorie baked goods priced about the same as their counterparts in traditional bakeries.

If you feel you've got a product that answers all these criteria, your next consideration is where to locate your store. Does the neighborhood matter? It does if you're going to couple a retail outlet with your kitchen location. But it might not if you are looking for a kitchen alone and will ship your products to customers' homes or to other retail locations. When the Miss Grace Lemon Cake Company was first purchased by Loretta Shine, its location in affluent Beverly Hills was important. If it had been located in a lower-middle-class neighborhood, chances of selling very many expensive lemon cakes over the counter would have been slight. However, the kitchen for The Thinnery is now located in Pacoima, definitely not a well-to-do section of town. The Bentons carefully pick locations for their retail outlets (often following the expansion of Weight Watchers franchises), but feel it would be wasteful to pay the inflated rents common in affluent areas of town .for the kitchen facility.

Ask yourself, too, if your product is likely to appeal particularly to a certain ethnic group or segment of society. If you want a bagel shop, for example, you'll undoubtedly do a lot better in a Jewish neighborhood than in a Scandinavian one. Keep these factors in mind when shopping for a location.

And take one final hint about location from Loretta Shine: "Before you sign the lease, have someone from the local health department come out and inspect your place. Make sure you won't have any grim surprises waiting for you later."

Will you be able to gain publicity for your product? Loretta Shine's initial business was boosted immensely by that television news spot. And Helen Benton, too, has benefitted from word-of-mouth among Weight Watchers members as well as from many local newspaper stories about her business. "We've never really spent much on advertising or publicity," she says. She's been lucky and she pegs her early days, "when we were still being seen more as a public service than as a business and when we got a lot of free publicity," as one of the highlights of The Thinnery's history.

If your product is unusual enough, or if you live in a small town, you can probably get free publicity quite easily. If not, be prepared to spend some money on advertising to let the public know your concern exists. And, if you're going to attempt mail-order sales, you'll have to set aside money for attractive color brochures (Loretta Shine's son took mouth-watering photos of cakes for her brochures) and price lists, postage costs, and advertising in magazines and newspapers. If no one knows you're around, you're not going to sell many cherry cheesecakes, no matter how wonderful they are.

And, before you decide a bakery business is for you, be sure that, according to Loretta Shine, "you can stand to be around food all day without turning into a tub. It's a horrible fight." Loretta stays slim, but not without a great deal of will power. "I don't enjoy cooking at home as much anymore," she says, "but I never get tired of eating it."

If having your own bakery has been your dream, don't despair because the old neighborhood store offering everything from hamburger buns to wedding cakes is disappearing under the bulldozer of the supermarket. With careful selection of an unusual, desirable, and limited line of baked products, you can still carve a place for your own bakery business in today's marketplace. Just start by using your baker's imagination.

3

Consider Catering

Do you love parties, weddings, and most other social gatherings? Do you have the talent to plan menus, cook the food, and organize events like these? Then catering may be the right food-related job for you. Even in today's competitive atmosphere, it's still possible to become a caterer on either a full- or part-time basis and earn money doing what you love.

Like any business, of course, catering has its drawbacks—usually related to money earned and hours worked—but it's one of the least expensive cooking businesses to begin. And it's also one that's most closely related to skills you have probably used at home. So take a look at two very different caterers and two very different businesses detailed here. Look at the pros and cons of catering as described by these women. And see if catering social events might be the right choice for you.

Helen Benton, who now owns The Thinnery, a low-calorie bakery products business (see Chapter 2), previously spent 12 years as a caterer. The way she began her catering career seems typical of many who go into the business. "It really started from a little hobby that got out of hand," she says. But, by the time she was ready to move on, Helen was employing 352 people and was catering parties for Hollywood stars like Marlo Thomas, Merv Griffin, and Shirley MacLaine. She points with pride to having catered Bob Hope's daughter's wedding, as well.

It all started back in the early 1960s when Helen joined the North Hollywood Junior Women's Club. "I found myself a committee of one doing luncheons for 400 people." That experience proved to her that she had the ability to organize major social events.

Shortly afterward, her neighbors became aware of Helen's cooking and organizational talents and began begging her to help them with card parties, bar mitzvahs, and weddings. "Before I knew it, it was more than I could handle," she recalls. "What it really amounted to was that I had too many friends."

Helen began to think about becoming a professional caterer instead of doing it as a favor. At first, she worked out of her home, using her family kitchen and a commercial refrigerator housed in her garage. But that was not legal and, in addition, her kitchen soon became too small for the kind of business she was building. "If you're talking about cooking for a couple of hundred people on a Saturday and a couple of hundred more on a Sunday, you've got to have space," she points out.

So Helen decided she needed a commercial kitchen. Since the business was expanding so rapidly, her husband, Bill, who was working in the construction industry, decided to join her company. They rented a 1000-square-foot store and began remodeling it. "The store was empty when we rented it," she recalls. "My husband, with his background in construction, put in the sink. We bought second-hand refrigerators and stoves and worktables and shelves." Because Bill knew all about building codes and permits, the Bentons had no trouble gaining a health department okay on their construction, and soon Helen Benton Personalized Parties was legal and in business.

Her catering service, because it was started in her home, never really required a large lump-sum investment, Helen says. "I got into it gradually. At first, I thought I'd work just long enough to buy portraits of my children—I had three by then—and then it was going to be just until I could buy a chafing dish. Then I had to have a second chafing dish, and after that I needed a table with two sides that pulled out to hold the chafing dishes. That's the way it went." She kept working and the business kept growing.

Helen bought a great deal of equipment over the years; something she does not advise that others do. "We ran into considerable expense buying our own equipment, and repairs and upkeep added a lot more. There are rental places that make a lot more sense, businesswise. But at the time, I wanted to have everything the way I wanted it. I didn't go into catering for the money, really. I ran things too much from the heart."

Helen Benton Personalized Parties grew largely through word-of-mouth recommendations and very soon other employees were needed. Helen, Bill, and their children could not handle things alone. So Helen ran ads in a community newspaper, asking for women interested in part-time kitchen work. "So many women, it seemed, wanted part-time jobs to get *out* of the kitchen," she says, "and I wanted to make sure they weren't the ones I hired." But her ads worked so well that she often got more than employees. "I joke that I got my best friends from those newspaper ads." She hired party cooks, kitchen cooks, and the people who actually handle the food at parties. "It's not like cooking the food at a restaurant," she points out. For example, catered foods are generally prepared in greater quantities and some items are only partially prepared in advance, then stored until the event.

When their business became even larger, the Bentons

merged with two young male caterers and changed the name of the new catering service to Carousel Catering. "The two men did more commercial work and I did the personalized parties," Helen says. Commercial work, she explains, might include something like a company supplying breakfast, lunch, and dinner for a work crew on location. A different, less elaborate kind of food is generally supplied, but more kitchen equipment, such as portable ovens and refrigerators, is required.

In 1973 the Bentons decided they'd had enough of catering and sold out to their partners. Why did they quit? Helen says, "I loved catering while I was doing it. I did things that there's no other way I could have done except through my catering business. How else do you get into Hugh Hefner's Playboy estate?" But there's a minus side to catering, too. "The lifestyle is weekends and nights and it's very demanding work. By that time, our children didn't want anything to do with it because they saw the life was difficult. They'd been busboys and dishwashers from day one.

"The catering business is very high-pressure, too," she adds. "It's a series of one-night stands. You've got somebody's wedding or something, and in four hours you've got to get it perfect. No excuses and no make-ups. The pressure is horrendous."

But, while she was doing it, Helen says she enjoyed it greatly. It was glamorous and exciting and very personally rewarding—most of the time. She started her own business, and watched it grow, and succeed. And, when she was ready to move on, her experience in catering held her in good stead while she created yet another food-related business.

Martha Stewart of Westport, Connecticut, caters from her home; she's installed a second, licensed, kitchen in the basement of her farm home. And it's there that she and a small staff prepare foods for parties entertaining as many as 2000 people.

Martha Stewart was formerly a stockbroker, so she began her catering career already well versed in business practices.

In fact, Martha was extremely successful as a stockbroker. When she left the business in 1973, she was earning $135,000 a year in commissions. But she decided she wanted to spend more time with her daughter, Alexis, who is now a teenager. And, in addition, the stock market had begun to decline. So Martha put her energies into restoring an old farmhouse she and her husband, Andrew, a publisher, had bought in Fairfield County, Connecticut. She planted gardens on their four acres of land, added chickens and roosters, and shortly thereafter began to teach cooking lessons for children 7 and 8 years old.

"I really didn't want to teach for the money," she says. "I just wanted to bring children my daughter's age into the house. I love children." Martha simply told the mothers of Alexis's classmates that she was going to offer cooking classes and the classes were immediately filled.

"Of course, I already had something of a reputation as a good cook," she says. Because of Andrew's profession, the Stewarts are required to entertain often and lavishly, so Martha quickly developed an ability to organize and cook for successful parties. She thought nothing of cooking and serving a dinner for twenty without help.

"I never had any formal training in cooking or nutrition," she says. "I learned from my mother and also I had a very generous expense account when I was a stockbroker." She had dined often at the best restaurants in the country, taking careful notice of the foods served.

Martha Stewart is something of a human dynamo. She found that staying at home, restoring an old farmhouse, running a small farm, and teaching children to cook was not enough to keep her busy and satisfied. So in 1976, with a $12,000 investment, she began a combination catering business and gourmet food shop. She built the shop, called The Market Basket, in a 600-square-foot space at the back of a friend's clothing store in Westport. It included both a kitchen and a small sales area.

Martha contracted with local homemakers to cook their special dishes at home and deliver them on a daily basis for sale at the shop. "The gourmet food shop was really a cooperative," she says. "The women had to have their kitchens licensed since requirements vary from community to community. Some built second kitchens in their homes if the laws prevented them from using their family kitchens." Many of these women had never worked for pay before and Martha is particularly proud of having introduced them to the business world. Several of them have since become caterers themselves. The women's special dishes were sold at a 50 percent markup and The Market Basket was an immediate success, earning the cooks a respectable wage from their cottage industry.

The shop rapidly outgrew its space, however, and Martha was unable to expand on The Market Basket site. So she decided to concentrate on her catering business and began building a second kitchen in her basement. She took some of the kitchen equipment from The Market Basket and bought other things secondhand. "Even my cupboards came from a friend who was remodeling her kitchen and buying new ones." The construction of the new kitchen included pouring a concrete floor; the Stewarts' home is so old that it had a dirt floor in the cellar. However, "even with the new floor," Martha says, "I don't think the kitchen cost more than $5000, and it's very big."

Martha's catering business has grown greatly due to word-of-mouth recommendations and the favorable publicity she's received. Her business is near the point where one person cannot handle it alone. "I'm very lucky because of where I live," she points out. "I'm close enough to New York City to cater parties there during the week. Almost nothing happens in New York on weekends, so then I do parties here in Fairfield County." That part of Connecticut is very affluent and quite socially oriented. So it's not unheard of for Martha to cater parties six or seven days a week.

A typical week in the spring of 1981 included:

Monday: a buffet for 250 at Sotheby Parke Bernet;

Tuesday: teaching two three-hour classes at a regional cooking center in Hartford;

Wednesday: a French cocktail party for 200 people;

Thursday: a reception for 700 at Sotheby Parke Bernet;

Friday: meetings at *Pepsico* to discuss catering an upcoming benefit for a local television station;

Saturday: a 50th birthday dinner party for 75.

A party catered by Martha Stewart means more than just good food. Her parties have become known, both for their decorations and the presentation of the food. For example, her hors d'oeuvres are carefully arranged on platters to look both appetizing and visually pleasing. Tables are decorated with fresh flowers or fruits and vegetables. And many of the foods she serves are grown on the Stewart farm, so they're literally fresh from the garden.

She prides herself on offering only top-quality, fresh foods. "I never skimp," she says. "Probably most people wouldn't know the difference between a cake-mix cake and one made from scratch, but I always assume they would. I see other caterers in the market putting cake mixes and canned vegetables in their baskets and I would never recommend them. I think a party deserves the best."

Her favorite parties? Those that offer the most challenge, often the largest. One she recalls well was a publicity party marking the publication of the book, *Faeries*. "We converted the U.S. Customs House in New York City into a fairyland and served 'midnight omelets' to a thousand people," she says. The party featured forest nymphs, mermaids, and waitresses wearing wings to enhance the fantasy atmosphere.

Martha is known for coming up with unusual foods around a specific theme. For example, she catered another large party at the Museum of American Folk Art in New York. It was the opening night of an antique show and the theme celebrated the Hudson River Valley. "We served foods all from the Hudson Valley, like apple fritters and buckwheat pancakes," she says. If that sounds like a difficult undertaking in the best of circumstances, Martha and her crew had to contend with the building's lack of a kitchen as well. "We had to rent and bring all kinds of portable equipment, like grills for the pancakes.

"The parties I like best," she says, "are those with the most challenge attached to them, not necessarily those given or attended by celebrities. For the menus, I just think a lot and try to come up with something unusual that I can offer using the facilities at hand. I don't have huge trucks with stoves and refrigerators like some caterers do, so I try to work with what's there."

Often that isn't much. At the time she was interviewed, Martha was about to cater a sit-down dinner for 400 at the former Doris Duke mansion in New York City. "And there's no stove, no refrigerator, not even a sink there, except the ones in the bathrooms." The dinner, in honor of retired diplomat Angier Biddle Duke, had a guest list which included Henry Kissinger and New York Governor Hugh Carey. The occasion required that Martha hire five cooks and 45 waiters as well as rent a variety of portable kitchen equipment to cook and refrigerate the food. But the size of the party and the building's lack of a kitchen didn't mean a skimpy bill of fare. Martha's menu included melon and proscuitto; lemon chicken; salad Nicoise; a cheese and watercress course; homemade walnut rolls; and a dessert of fresh strawberries in raspberry sauce.

The help Martha hires for such large parties includes "a wonderful list of people, many of them unemployed actors and actresses. They work as cooks or servers, depending on their talents." She also employs several part-time cooks at her Westport home kitchen, one of them former top fashion model Dorian Leigh, who works two days a week. Another employee does all the grocery shopping under Martha's direction.

Martha's own talents now are spent planning parties and menus, setting prices, hiring and supervising employees, doing some of the cooking, and taking care of her garden.

"I use a lot of food from my garden," she says. "For example, I'm doing a party for House Beautiful magazine. It's a retirement party for someone who's worked there for years. Much of the food, the mint and herbs and the flowers are all from my garden." With her busy catering schedule, however, it's hard to find much time to be a gardener. "I spent most of Memorial Day weekend in the garden," she confesses. That's the weekend she says she "took off," except for a party she gave on Saturday night.

Martha Stewart's parties are fairly high-priced, costing between $10 and $45 a person for food only. She says that she has a "secret formula" by which she prices them, but basically she figures out how much a party will cost her, considering the menu and the number of people, and adds on the amount of profit she feels she can charge. That amount varies from party to party. "I do all the auctions for Sotheby Parke Bernet, for example, sometimes three or four a week, so I feel I can charge them differently than I might an individual for whom I might do only one party. You learn what to charge through experience." Martha urges caterers to charge enough to be fair to themselves, but often finds that they do not; too many lack her keen business sense. "Some of the women who work for me cater parties on the side and they show me their contracts. Their prices are sometimes way too low. I see that they'll be lucky to make a dollar an hour for their own time. No one should do a party for free."

Martha's workdays are often at least 18 hours long. "If you count the catering business, working on a book that I'm writing, taking care of the garden, and changing the beds." In addition, she has the entertainment obligations inherent in being a publisher's wife. Sometimes those events conflict with her catering, but she's learned to take that in stride. "Luckily, people seem to be interested in what I'm doing. Catering has become fashionable; it's considered glamorous now. At parties, people often turn the conversation around to the catering business and ask me what my favorite party was and what I served." When guests visit her Connecticut farmhouse, they sometimes even pitch in and peel potatoes if Martha's working on a party deadline. "I've become much more calm about that kind of thing now. In the beginning, I was a nervous wreck," she says.

Now that she's well established, Martha Stewart's catering

business seldom sees a slow period. "The last six months have been so busy," she says. "Even in January we had 13 big parties. And I was already booked for all of June by the end of April." She's now turning down business because she's too busy to handle it.

Most caterers would love to have Martha Stewart's problem: more potential customers than she can handle. In five years in business, she's turned a cottage industry into one of the most successful individually owned catering businesses in the country.

Maybe you'd like to be in Martha Stewart's shoes, or perhaps you'd like to have a smaller catering business. Before you take out an ad announcing to the world that you've become a caterer, however, consider for a moment what's really involved in the business and what you have to offer it.

The first thing you might examine is your ability as a hostess. Do you have vast experience in giving parties? Martha Stewart was used to hosting New York's high society in her roles as a stockbroker and as the wife of a publisher; Helen Benton had given dozens of parties on a somewhat smaller scale. And each of these women used her social contacts to help her get started in the catering business. Look at your own social contacts. Do you know people who hire or recommend caterers? Your friends are likely to be your best advertisement until you are well establshed, so scrutinize them to see just how much help they can be to you.

Think about the area in which you live as well. What kind of entertaining do people in your town generally do? Are large catered parties the rule or are most people more inclined to stick to small dinners and card parties, reserving their use of caterers to an occasional wedding or graduation dinner? If your area is more like the latter, it doesn't necessarily mean that you shouldn't become a caterer. It simply means that you should understand what you're getting into and what level of success you can reasonably expect.

Ask yourself what's special about *your* parties. Is it your food? Or is it a special atmosphere, the people who attend them, the decorations? Some of these things, of course, are the province of the caterer and some are not. As a caterer, you can provide unusual and tantalizing foods. You can suggest party themes, costumes, and decorations. But you cannot supply interesting guests crucial to a party's success. Are the things for which a caterer is responsible the things you do best?

Take the decorations, for example. Among the parties Martha Stewart has catered have been ones using themes of a Mexican fiesta and a Victorian country fair. Do you have the imagination and skill to suggest and supervise the manufacture of decorations for events like these? Martha often hires a designer to help with this part of a special party and then adds the designer's fees to her own.

The financial investment necessary to create any small business is a consideration in catering as well, of course. Many caterers attempt to begin in their home kitchens. But that *is* illegal, and they could find themselves making a much larger financial investment by breaking the law than they intended. They not only risk being fined by the health department but, because working from an unlicensed kitchen means they have no insurance, they could also lose a large sum in a lawsuit if anyone were to become ill after eating their food. Therefore, it is imperative that you check into the health department requirements in your city before plunging into a home catering business. Check the appendix of this book for more informational resources.

There are middle grounds between building a commercial kitchen of your own and breaking the law by cooking in your family kitchen, however. Some caterers, for instance, rent restaurant kitchens during hours they're not being used by the restaurant chefs. Is there a small restaurant near you that's open only in the evenings? If so, try approaching the owner about renting space there in the mornings. Other little-used commercial kitchens that might be for rent a few hours a week could be found in churches, synagogues, and social clubs.

With some parties, you might be able to do all your cooking on the premises of the party, thus by-passing many legal and financial problems. It *is* legal for you to cook in your client's kitchen; there, you are considered a cook for hire. Although this means keeping your menu simple and specializing in foods that can be prepared at the last minute, it could be a temporary solution until you can build or buy your own licensed kitchen.

If you do decide to build a commercial kitchen, consider building it in your home if you own one, like Martha Stewart did. Obviously, this would save you the rental on a separate space. This is particularly practical in the large homes common in the East and North. A basement could be an ideal space for a new kitchen, as could an unused garage or guest house. By using secondhand kitchen equipment and a few other cost-cutting measures, you might be able to do nearly as well as Martha Stewart did; she paid less than $5000 for a substantial and legal kitchen space in her home.

If you're considering building a second kitchen at home, however, be sure to check your local zoning ordinances to see if it's legal for you to run a catering business from your home. And call the health department about regulations before you spend a dime on construction. With help from the authorities in the beginning, you're much less likely to run into trouble later on.

Finally, if you decide you must have a commercial kitchen outside your home that's exclusively yours, try to do that as inexpensively as possible. First, look for an existing kitchen that's for sale. Perhaps another caterer is trying to sell his business. One Los Angeles caterer, for example, worked out of a restaurant kitchen at first and then bought out another caterer who had a licensed kitchen of her own.

If you rent, remember, there's no real reason to pay the inflated rates charged in the best parts of town for your kitchen space. Your clients never need come to your kitchen. You go to them. So, in the interest of saving rent money you can undoubtedly use for something else, consider a less fashionable address for your facility.

Martha Stewart built the kitchen at The Market Basket for $12,000. Today, it would cost somewhat more, of course, and the price will vary according to where you live and the costs of kitchen appliances and fixtures, construction supplies, and labor. To keep your costs down, look for used kitchen equipment. Both Stewart and Helen Benton made substantial savings by doing that and neither regretted her decision.

If you're serious about becoming a professional caterer, there will be certain cooking utensils you'll have to buy: oversized cooking pots and pans, large food mixers, mixing bowls big enough for a wedding cake batter, etc. But it's possible to find many of these items used, too. If you hear that a local restaurant or bakery is going out of business, for example, contact the owner and ask what he's planning to do with any equipment you could use. He may be delighted to sell it to you used, at a great savings.

Avoid buying any but entirely necessary catering equipment, however. That includes anything that you won't be using on a daily basis and that could be rented more economically. Helen Benton still regrets having bought as much equipment as she did and recommends that no one follow her lead in this department. Rental agencies can provide all kinds of cooking and refrigerating items that you'll use only on an occasional basis. For Martha Stewart's Hudson River Valley party, for instance, she rented portable gas and electric griddles. To buy them would have been prohibitively expensive and she probably would have had little use for them at subsequent parties. Owning your own exotic equipment brings with it the problems of keeping it in working order and finding storage space for it, too. So get to know your local rental agencies and become acquainted with the items they offer and their rental rates.

A vehicle to transport your foods and decorations to your parties is also a necessity. If you own a family station wagon, that's a good start and it can keep you in business for awhile.

The amount of income you can expect to earn from a catering business will vary greatly, depending on a number of factors. In order to make money, the most important thing to learn is how to price your parties fairly so your customers are satisfied and you make a good profit. Most caterers compute how much the party will cost them by adding in such elements as the cost of food, hired labor, transportation, a portion of their overhead, decorations, and rental fees for items such as cooking equipment and dishes. Then they tack on a reasonable profit for their time and investment. This latter amount depends partially on what your competition is charging for their parties, something you can probably find out at least in general with a few telephone calls. It also depends on the kind of town in which you live. If you're going to be catering parties for the very wealthy or for movie stars, as Martha Stewart and Helen Benton have done, you can obviously charge more for a unique party than if you work for people with average incomes. If you're planning a corporate extravaganza, you can add on a larger markup than if you're doing a wedding for a family on a strict budget. As Stewart says, you'll learn how to price your events through experience. Just remember to add in enough for yourself so that you're running a business, not a charity. Don't, Helen Benton says, run your business "from the heart." You're in business to make money. And if you don't make money, you won't be in business very long.

Be aware and plan for the fact that every catering business takes time to establish itself. When you consider financing, be sure to include enough to cover your living expenses until you become known and your business expands. It's likely that your reputation will grow as you get more clients, but those first few can be hard to come by. Tell everyone you know that you're opening a catering business. Consider a listing in the Yellow Pages of your telephone book. Have business cards printed and pass them out everywhere. Do what you can to gather publicity for your enterprise. For example, try offering a lower price to cater a charity function that will give you a chance to show off your capabilities to many people who hire caterers. You may get a mention in your local newspaper at the same time.

As Martha Stewart says, "You can't just call people up and ask if they're planning to have any parties you can cater." So your reputation and word-of-mouth advertising are vital to your business. Use whatever business contacts you may have to get contracts to cater business events. A vital element in Martha's business, for example, is those three or four auctions a week that she caters for Sotheby Parke Bernet. If you can obtain a similar contract in your town, your catering business will have a strong base from which to expand.

An additional piece of financial advice from these professional caterers: be firm about demanding deposits from your customers. It's always possible that something can happen to cancel one of your parties. People get sick, a relative dies, whatever. If you don't have a deposit, you're likely to be left with food you've paid for and no way to recover your costs. A fairly standard arrangement is to ask for 50 percent of the party's price upfront, and the other 50 percent on the day of the party. If you have to pay out a substantial amount of cash in advance for such things as equipment rentals, you may wish to ask for more than 50 percent as a deposit.

As your business grows or as you begin to cater larger and larger parties, you'll soon have to hire occasional help, but this should not be difficult in most areas of the country. You may not live in a town where out-of-work actors are crying for such jobs, as Martha Stewart does, but you can undoubtedly find college students and housewives eager to earn some extra money. Try calling your local college's student placement office for waiters and waitresses. Or put an ad in your local newspaper, like Helen Benton did, asking for people who want part-time jobs working with food. To determine what pay rates prevail in your area of the country, check the want ads, ask other caterers what they pay their help, call employment agencies for information (the free service run by your state employment department can be particularly helpful).

Catering, like all businesses, has disadvantages as well as advantages, of course. Helen Benton got out of it because she tired of the constant nights and weekends the work typically demands. Before you decide to become a caterer, ask yourself whether or not you will like working those hours. How will your family react if you're working every weekend and several nights as well? Because of the unusual working hours it demands, catering can be a difficult business to have in a two-career marriage unless both spouses are involved in it.

Your income from catering may be quite seasonal, too, unless you're lucky enough to enjoy a level of success like Martha Stewart's. January, for example, is traditionally a very slow month for caterers. The Christmas and New Year's holidays are over. People are tired of parties and have probably spent as much money on entertaining as they can afford for awhile. In her first year in the business, one new caterer found January a particularly discouraging month. "In January, I thought I might not make it," she said. "I knew in my head that January was going to be slow, but the experience of watching the checkbook balance go down, down, down and no business coming in was really discouraging." February, however, brought her Valentine's Day parties and "almost spring" parties . . . and new hope. Particularly when you're new in the catering business, you have to be financially able to weather these seasonal lows. And you have to be able to weather them emotionally as well.

Catering can be hard work: toting groceries; standing for hours over a chopping board; lifting huge pots of soup; carrying the prepared foods. This kind of work takes physical strength and stamina. And, on the day of the party, you may well have to work an 18-hour day and still be bright and smiling for your clients and their guests.

Martha Stewart points out, "It takes a lot of energy and you really have to be tireless. You always have to perform. You have a huge obligation when you contract to do someone's party. It's a lot to cope with."

As Helen Benton adds, if you're doing someone's wedding, it's too important to them to allow for your mistakes. If your busboy doesn't show up, you bus the dishes yourself. If the day is hot and humid, you find a way to keep the icing on the wedding cake from melting. If the market is out of lettuce, you find something else that will do the job just as well.

Catering demands a particularly flexible kind of personality. You have to be able to cope creatively with a crisis. It can be a high-pressure business, but it's also glamorous and fun. Catering can put you in touch with the most exciting social events in your town. Indeed, you can actually be responsible for them and, in the process, become something of a celebrity yourself. It can also be tremendously personally rewarding to have a satisfied and happy customer thank you for making his wedding, or golden anniversary, or child's bar mitzvah, one of the most memorable days of his life.

So if you love parties and think you'd like to be giving lots of them for others as well as yourself . . . consider catering.

4

The Teaching Cook

Have you a flair for the dramatic? Do you enjoy being with other people as much as you enjoy cooking? If you can answer "Yes" to both of these questions and also want a part-time income, teaching others to cook may be an excellent way for you to cash in on your cooking skills.

Becoming a cooking instructor takes little in the way of either financial investment or professional training. That's not to say that you can't spend a fortune opening a lavishly equipped cooking school or training at the Cordon Bleu if you desire, but that's not necessary. Literally thousands of good cooks earn money teaching others their self-taught food preparation skills from home kitchens, in adult education classes, and in special cooking schools. And this aspect of the food business has room for all levels of involvement, from having fun and earning a few extra dollars by teaching a class or two a week, to setting up and running a complete cooking school.

While teaching cooking can be fun, it's definitely not the most lucrative of the cooking-related occupations. It can be, however, a wonderful stepping stone to other better-paying positions in the field. Cooking teachers have gone on to write cookbooks, demonstrate their skills on their own television cooking shows, become caterers, open their own restaurants, and so on. And teaching is a great way to try a cooking business on for size to see how you like it before making the greater monetary and time commitments other cooking careers require.

Marlene Sorosky of Tarzana, California, started as a home-based cooking teacher. Over a period of several years, she expanded her business into a full-fledged cooking school and gourmet shop called Marlene Sorosky's Cooking Center School and Shop. She's also the author of a cookbook.

"I started teaching cooking through my children's school PTA," she recalls. "They had a gourmet club to raise money and I started demonstrating to a small group how a food was prepared and then serving it to them for lunch." The first year Marlene worked with the PTA as a "demonstration mother" and then the second year she took over as head of the entire club. But, ironically, the club became too successful. "It got so big that we couldn't handle all the members," she says. "When we closed it down, we had 200."

That was in 1970, when Marlene had four children under the age of seven, one of them an infant. But she still wanted to do something more than be a wife and mother. Then, as a result of her PTA stint, she got a job offer. "The owner of a gourmet cooking shop who had heard of me called and said he wanted to add a cooking school to his shop and asked if I wanted to run it." Marlene, in her search for something to occupy her extra time, had thought of beginning work toward a master's degree in social work. "But my husband said that there were so many social workers and that I was good at teaching people to cook, so why didn't I give that a try instead." So she began planning to become a professional cooking teacher, drawing on a combination of her skills with food and earlier college training in elementary education. She planned the recipes she would teach and worked on her presentation style. But then the bottom dropped out. The gourmet shop owner changed his mind and Marlene was left without a job after all.

"I had prepared psychologically to become a cooking teacher, so I thought, why not do it out of my home?" Marlene was fortunate to have a large house with a kitchen that would accommodate a good-sized group of observers. "I started with 12 students and taught once or twice a week, finally building up to 80 students." Marlene never had to advertise. Word of her cooking expertise spread as a result of her PTA involvement and as her early students told others about her classes.

After eight years of teaching cooking in her home kitchen, she was making a very respectable income. She says that, by the late 1970s, she was teaching small groups totalling 40 students each week and charging each of them $15 a lesson, earning a gross income of $600 a week. From that, she had to deduct few expenses other than the food she used. She'd spent almost nothing setting up shop because she used her home kitchen and she was able to teach while her children were at school. "I held my classes in the morning, and by the time my kids got home from school, I'd cleaned up and you'd never even know I'd had a class there."

It was too good to last, however. After teaching from her home for a full eight years, Marlene got a letter from the city saying her house wasn't zoned for a business and she'd have to stop teaching. "I was threatened with 60 days in jail and a $500 fine if I continued to teach in my home." Marlene thinks an irate neighbor turned her in, a risk one takes teaching as she did. So, suddenly she was without a job again.

She really didn't feel ready to set up a business elsewhere, but she was afraid she'd lose her momentum if she waited until she felt ready. "My hand was forced by that letter," she says, "and I felt I'd have to move quickly whether I was ready or not.

"I thought I'd just rent a store somewhere and teach there," she says, but she found it wasn't that easy. "I researched cooking schools and found out that you can't really make any money unless you teach eight hours a day, six days a week (the hours a store would normally be open) and that's physically impossible." Marlene knew she would have to pay just as much rent as if she had a dress shop or a bakery, for instance, but the cooking school would earn her less money.

She decided to combine her cooking school with a related business in order to make full use of the store space she would have to rent and remodel. "I thought a gourmet shop was a natural second project," she says. "I would teach people to use the equipment that the shop carried. They'd be buying it somewhere, so why not from my shop?"

She had a viable idea and began planning for it. But Marlene had to change, too. She'd been a combination housewife and cooking teacher and now suddenly she had to become a businesswoman, too. "I changed psychologically when I started planning the store," she says. "It was not a hobby anymore. There was much more pressure."

She had to find a space she could afford to rent and that had adequate parking adjacent to it. She finally selected 2000 square feet in a shopping center close to a freeway entrance. Her rent was $1400 a month.

The space needed extensive remodeling to make it into her idea of a gourmet shop and cooking school, so she drew up plans for that. Then she had to borrow money. "And I'd never owed anything before. That made me very nervous."

Marlene began with a $50,000 bank loan which she was able to obtain, in part, because, of the seven executives of her bank, "six had heard of me and my home cooking school." She began construction of a space that included shelves for her merchandise; a checkout-counter area; and a large, airy kitchen where she could teach cooking to students who would participate as they learned.

While the construction for her new shop was underway, Marlene began buying her store's stock. "I went to see the wholesalers every day for two months and just asked myself what I thought I'd need to stock the store," she says. Marlene decided she would not stock any item she wouldn't use herself, so her merchandise is somewhat more select than that found in many similar stores. Even so, she says, she "overbought and undercapitalized." She went back to the bank and borrowed another $40,000.

Then the store construction went 30 days over schedule, delaying the opening date. "The problem there was that I'd already taken delivery on most of my stock," Marlene says. "I'd bought it on 30-day credit and by the time we opened I already owed money and hadn't sold anything yet." During the first month she was in business, Marlene found herself scraping up payments for her creditors from each day's receipts.

The beginning was very difficult. Marlene felt she should have had more financial advice, a common complaint of new business owners. She also found that she couldn't do everything herself, so she hired a man to run the gourmet shop for her while she ran the cooking school. And the business affected her family life, too. "It left my kids in a difficult position. They were angry and they missed me, but my heart was really here in the business. I saw it as a temporary sacrifice until we got going successfully. But it took a full year before I could see some equilibrium between my business and my family life."

It was tough both physically, in sheer numbers of hours spent setting up what amounted to two businesses at the same time, and also psychologically. Those business loans really bothered Marlene and "I kept having dreams at night that I was drowning," she says. She was very lucky, though. Her business took off and became successful very quickly. She was able to pay off her $50,000 loan during her first year in business, an accomplishment of which she's very proud.

Ironically, Marlene's students now are not the same people she had taught in her home. Those students, she says, were all other housewives who became quite threatened by her foray into the professional world. "As long as I was a housewife like them, who just happened to make a little money on the side, things were fine. But when I opened the store, they didn't come. At first my classes dropped off, but I live in a big city and there are plenty of other people here who want to learn cooking. I now have 8000 on my mailing list." She's also featured once a month on a local restaurant critic's television show, so that exposure brings in many potential students.

After a couple of years in business, Marlene Sorosky's Cooking Center School and Shop is an unqualified success, although the gourmet shop brings in more income than the cooking school does. The shop features all kinds of cooking-related items from spices to pots and pans, from graters and spoons to food processors. She employs 12 people now, up from the five she began with.

Marlene now teaches five classes a week, with 24 students in each class. Her classes change periodically but a typical sampling includes Menus for Entertaining, Men in the Kitchen, a six-part course in the Basics of Cooking, a Chili Cook-off, and two classes in how to use a food processor (an item that is for sale in the gourmet shop, of course).

She also offers classes by guest instructors with a particular cooking expertise. These include pastry making, Chinese cooking, northern Italian cooking, and "vegetable wizardry." Students pay from $20 for the Chili Cook-off to $350 for an in-depth cooking workshop by guest instructor Barbara Kafka, who usually teaches with James Beard in the New York City area. The fees charged depend both upon the instructor and the number of lessons in a series.

Marlene's career as a cooking teacher and store owner has brought her more than financial success. She's also becoming a local celebrity. (This often happens with top cooking teachers.) She was selected to assist Julia Child at some of her charity demonstrations on the West Coast and even cooked dinner for the great chef in her shop one night. "I didn't feel intimidated at all," Marlene says. "Julia's not the kind of person who intimidates you. She's very easy going and helpful to other people and I treasure her advice."

Marlene Sorosky is justifiably proud of what she's accomplished with her business, but she admits it's been very hard on her. What she'd like now is some time off to savor her success.

Martha Stewart, the Westport, Connecticut, caterer, earns a second income teaching in a few cooking schools in her home state. "I teach in regional cooking schools in Hartford, Westport, and Darien," she says. One such school is even located in the back of a bookstore.

"I teach a wide variety of subjects and I try never to repeat myself," Martha says. Because of the demands of her catering business, her teaching is limited to occasional three-hour sessions instead of courses that meet weekly. That doesn't result in any lack of students, however.

She describes one of her recent courses: "It was on summer entertaining and it included the organization of a party from start to finish, ten of my best hors d'oeuvre recipes, the presentation of the food, the decorations, everything. I usually teach one three-hour session in the morning and another three-hour session in the evening."

Unlike Marlene's students, Martha's do not participate during class time. One advantage for the instructor in this style of teaching is that it's possible to include more students at a time. Martha is paid a percentage of the cooking school's gross receipts from each of her courses. "They generally charge from $35 to $45 a person for one of my courses," she says, "and the enrollment is about 25 to 30 people."

Although teaching six hours of cooking in one day is physically and emotionally draining, it's lucrative for Martha in terms of the time she devotes to that part of her professional life. As a guest instructor, she's responsible only for planning her lesson, teaching her courses, and keeping in touch with the cooking school administration. She also takes no real financial risks teaching this way. She earns less if a class has a low enrollment, but there's no way that she can *lose* money.

All in all, Martha Stewart finds teaching her cooking skills on an occasional basis both a financially and emotionally rewarding second occupation.

Holly Torath, too, teaches cooking as a second job along with a fledgling catering business based in Beverly Hills, California. As a public school teacher, Holly taught cooking to her special education classes to help the children learn, not only to cook, but also to develop math and speech skills. While teaching in the public schools, she began to give private cooking lessons to adults interested in special kinds of cooking such as breads, soups, and vegetable dishes. "Most of the time I would go to someone else's house to teach a small group and I would charge according to what I thought my time was worth and what the food cost."

Now, she's teaching in adult education classes sponsored by two local school districts and for another city's parks and recreation department. "I'm paid by the hour for the classes and for my preparation time and reimbursed for the food costs," she explains. Teaching these courses provides only a supplemental income for Holly, who is a vegetarian, but it does have one definite advantage: she knows precisely how much she will earn from her teaching time. There are absolutely no financial risks for her and even the class enrollment has no effect on her income.

Holly got her jobs because the public agencies she works for heard about her and asked her to teach. Good vegetarian cooks are rare and Holly is in constant demand because she offers a combination of cooking ability and the teaching skills she honed in the public schools.

Her classes are generally taught on weekday evenings, so they don't conflict with her catering jobs. There is some preparation time for each class she teaches and that time, too, is worked around her catering schedule.

"You have to buy your own food when you teach," she says. But that chore can be combined with shopping trips for her catering business. Other pre-class planning involves deciding what foods she will prepare, and sometimes even partially preparing some of the dishes, "maybe chopping onions or something that's time-consuming and boring to watch," she says. Occasionally, too, a food takes longer to prepare than the time allowed in class, so she must have a finished product to show to her students. One special vegetarian hors d'oeuvre recipe, for example, "tastes horrible when it's just prepared. It has to sit for 24 hours for the flavors to blend and then it's wonderful." So, she makes a recipe the day before the class for her students to sample and also demonstrates the preparation steps during the class session.

Holly says there's a definite difference in size between her adult education classes and those she teaches in private homes. The former usually range in size from 12 to 20 and the latter run only about six or eight students. Because she teaches in a variety of settings, Holly has to be able to vary her teaching style according to the facilities available and the number of students enrolled. In a private home, for example, she will demonstrate how to make a dish. In one of her adult education classes, however, when space and facilities are available, her students will participate by preparing the food along with her.

Holly finds her public classes particularly interesting because about a third of her students are men. And they're often among the most enthusiastic.

For Holly, an additional payoff from teaching is that it adds to her reputation as a cook, and that ultimately helps her fledgling catering business to grow. She finds potential customers among her students, and they also spread word of her abilities to their friends. Every bit of favorable publicity she gathers, from whatever source, makes her eventual success as a caterer that much more likely.

As you can see from the experiences of Marlene Sorosky, Martha Stewart, and Holly Torath, there are many different kinds of jobs available to teach cooking, ranging from something that's just slightly more than a hobby all the way to running a good-sized business like Marlene's.

Teaching does take more than just being a good cook, however. It also requires certain personality traits.

You have to be a bit of a showman. Talking in front of groups of people can't bother you. In fact, it helps if you love to show off your skills to others.

Marlene Sorosky and Holly Torath were both trained as schoolteachers, although Marlene never used her teaching credentials in the classroom. Martha Stewart was formerly a stockbroker, a profession that requires top-level communications skills. You don't need to have formal training in speech or teaching, of course, but you should feel comfortable with the concept of speaking to a class and demonstrating a skill clearly.

All three of these women are attractive as well as personable, which isn't mandatory, but doesn't hurt, either. People want to be entertained while they learn.

Holly Torath also points out that it's important to be well organized if you want to be a cooking instructor. "You need a good sense of time to do this," she says. "For instance, you have to know how much you can really do in an hour's time." If you plan to demonstrate how to bake an apple pie, for example, and you've got only an hour to do it, you obviously cannot start from scratch when the class assembles and expect the students to be able to taste your creation before the bell rings. You probably will need to have your apples sliced before class convenes and you'll need a second, already baked pie ready for sampling during the class session as well.

You will have to bring something special to your classes, too. Marlene Sorosky is well aware of this. She types up recipe cards for the dishes she's created and gives one to each student. And she also teaches both basic and specialized courses with a personalized flair that makes them both informative and fun. "I ask myself why someone would pay me $25 for a class when they could buy five cookbooks for that price," she says. "So they have to get something out of my class that they can't get out of cookbooks." That something is a social, entertaining morning or afternoon.

When she teaches, Martha Stewart is careful not to repeat the same anecdotes from one class to the next, a strain on her, but entertaining for her students. That way a student is likely to return again and again to take more of Martha's courses.

If you've got the basic skills and interests necessary to become a cooking teacher, think about starting small. One reason this is a great occupation is that you can try it out and see if you like it before committing yourself to lots of time or money. Holly Torath says, "I could see someone teaching in the evenings and combining it with a full-time job somewhere else." So, even if you're employed now, try teaching a course or two before you decide on a complete career change.

Be sure to check your local zoning laws if you're considering teaching in your home. Will you be breaking your city's laws if you run a business in your home? If so, and you simply want a chance to build up your reputation and try teaching to see if you like it, consider charging only enough to cover your food costs. You won't earn an income, but you won't break the law, either.

Check with your local health department, too. Regulations for cooking schools vary in different parts of the country. While Marlene Sorosky was not in violation of any health department rules when she taught in her home kitchen, that may not have been the case had she lived elsewhere in the country. Marlene serves as the secretary-treasurer of the National Association of Cooking Schools and she says that there will probably soon be codes covering cooking schools, although there are none now.

"You need insurance," she points out, "but no license or permit to run a cooking school." Insurance is important not only to cover a customer who might become ill after eating food in your establishment, but also to protect you in case a student is injured. (This type of insurance is for all cooking businesses.) With cooking students, injuries such as sliced fingers and burns are fairly common. If you are hired by a school district or established cooking school to teach in their facilities, however, you won't need insurance. Their policies will cover you.

If you'd like to teach in such an adult education class, you needn't wait for your school district or parks and recreation department to contact you. Find out who hires instructors and contact him or her. If there are no adult education cooking courses in your area, outline one you could teach and propose it. High-school home-economics classrooms usually have several cooking stations that are unused in the evenings, so they make wonderful places to hold evening cooking courses for adults.

If you'd like to teach in an established private cooking school, the same procedure applies. You're more likely to be hired, of course, if you have a known reputation in some other field of cooking (if you're a successful caterer, or you have your own restaurant, for instance), or if you have an unusual specialty, such as Holly Torath's expertise in vegetarian cooking. Your specialty shouldn't be too obscure, however. Your income will probably depend on how many students you attract, so you'll want full classes. And so will the cooking school. Once you've been hired to teach one cooking class, expand your abilities so you can teach others. You want repeat customers and you'll need to offer a variety of courses to get them.

If you dream of your own private cooking school, take some pointers from Marlene Sorosky's research and experience. It's almost impossible to make a profit from a cooking school alone unless you pay almost no rent for your facility. So consider coupling your school with a gourmet shop, as Marlene did, or holding your classes in a catering kitchen or restaurant kitchen. Do whatever you can to keep your rental expenses down, thus pushing your profits up.

For most cooking instructors, it's a part-time income. If that's all you require, you may have found your niche. If you need more now or in the future, however, try to build your reputation in this area of cooking so that you can expand into others more easily. Marlene Sorosky is now not only a cooking teacher, but the owner of a gourmet shop and a cookbook author as well. Martha Stewart is also a caterer and author of a book on entertaining. In the future, she hopes to teach cooking on her own television show. Holly Torath, who is still just starting out, is a caterer as well as a cooking teacher.

No matter how you decide to begin your career as a cooking teacher, one thing is of utmost importance to your success—your reputation. Students must believe that you can teach them something they can't get from a cookbook and that no one else can teach it quite as well. That means you have to become known.

Luckily, since teaching cooking is usually seen to be as much an educational pursuit as a commercial one, gaining media publicity for your courses will probably be much easier than getting the same coverage for a bakery business, restaurant, or other food-related business. Many newspapers will list scheduled cooking courses in their current events columns free of charge. If you teach for an adult education department, ask the public relations people handling publicity to include your name as well as your course title in their news releases and printed materials. Take out ads, if necessary. Post flyers announcing your courses (including your name and possibly even your photograph) on bulletin boards where people buy food and cooking equipment. Create a mailing list as you progress. Marlene Sorosky started with a small mailing list and now she has names of more than 8000 people catalogued according to their cooking interests.

These tips will help people come to know you and to think of you as a top cooking instructor and foods expert. And that will help your teaching income grow.

5

Setting Up a Specialty Shop

Although you may not realize it, running your own food store can call upon your cooking abilities nearly as much as running your own bakery or catering service. Since you can't really compete successfully with the neighborhood Safeway or A&P (even the old mom and pop stores are getting stiff competition from such chains as 7-Eleven), setting up your own food store, like setting up most food businesses today, means one thing: specialization. And when you have a specialized store, your customers are likely to ask your advice on preparing the foods you sell.

Specialized food stores come in a variety of descriptions: ethnic grocery stores where good cooks can buy such items as Chinese vegetables or Italian spices; health food stores; wine and cheese shops; produce markets. Most of the small ones have carved out a niche for themselves; they're not really in competition with either the supermarkets or the all-night convenience stores. Their customers often travel many miles to buy the products they offer. And, because they travel a distance and probably pay a slightly higher price for what these stores offer, customers expect more than an automated checkout service. They look for the owner's advice and knowledge about food, as well.

Many food store owners today started their businesses because of their love for food as much as their desire to earn an income. If they sell Mexican foods, for instance, chances are they also sell the appropriate cookbooks and enjoy advising their customers on how to prepare each and every product on their shelves. Owners of cheese shops know the origin and taste of each cheese they sell. If a customer wants to make a marvelous fondue, for instance, the cheese store owner can advise her which Swiss cheeses are made from goats' milk and which from cows', as well as which wine's taste will blend best with the flavor of the cheeses. The proprietor of a coffee and tea store will know the taste of each kind he sells and will be able to advise his customers on grinding each bean and steeping each tea leaf.

Opening your own food store is one of the more ambitious projects in this book, largely because it requires a heavy financial investment in stock as well as rental of a relatively large store space. But, with the right idea for an unusual store, good business advice and enough financing, you, too, can be the owner of a special new food store.

Sandra Gooch of Los Angeles, proprietor of Mrs. Gooch's Natural Food Store, is a wonderful example of a person who took her personal interest in food and built it into a successful business. Started in 1976, by 1981 Mrs. Gooch's was grossing more than $7 million a year in its two locations (Mar Vista and Hermosa Beach) and was planning to open a third store in nearby Northridge.

It's a very special health food store because *everything* Sandy stocks is completely natural. Her products contain no chemical additives, no preservatives, no artificial coloring, no white flour, and no refined sugar.

Sandy's interest in natural foods evolved through dire

necessity. And it's this interest that she parlayed into a successful store that her critics said could never work. Up until 1974, Sandy was a typical school teacher with no particular health problems save one allergy, to peanut products. Like most working wives and mothers, she utilized a variety of convenience foods in her home cooking, foods that were laden with additives of all kinds.

Then a head cold suddenly changed her life. Sandy's doctor prescribed tetracycline, a commonly used antibiotic. A few days later, she says, "I thought I was dying. Shaking, severe chest pains, head spinning. It seemed like a heart attack." Sandy was rushed to UCLA Hospital, where doctors were unable to find any cause for her unusual symptoms. Eventually, her symptoms subsided and Sandy resumed her life as usual.

Two weeks later, she was again given tetracycline, this time for an eye infection and within minutes, "my body began to react violently and it didn't stop for three solid days." She was sent to Scripps Institute, and baffled doctors there, too. "They were observing my symptoms," she says, "and then on the fifth day a violent attack was controlled in the final moments by a shot of Benadryl. It literally saved my life."

Sandy's father, a scientist, began to think that her condition was being irritated by the foods she was eating. The last thing she'd ingested before the near-fatal attack at Scripps, for example, was a can of diet soda and he theorized that it had contained something to which Sandy was allergic.

When she returned home, the mysterious attacks continued and Sandy and her father became certain that her body was rejecting certain foods. "We read, wrote letters, asked thousands of questions," she says, "and all the while, I continued to experience those terrifying attacks. In fact, even the first meal I cooked upon returning from Scripps triggered the frightening experience again."

Through their research, which lasted for more than a year, Sandy and her father became aware of many food facts, such as a state law requiring that out-of-state chickens be dipped in tetracycline, the very antibiotic that had triggered her initial violent allergy. That homecoming meal had consisted in part of, you guessed it, chicken. "Disenchantment set in," Sandy says, "the more we uncovered about the chemicals in and on foods the American masses eat, and for me, how it affected my body."

Another thing they learned was that the diet soda she'd drunk before her near-fatal attack contained bromelated vegetable oil, an ingredient that acts in the body to instantly reduce antihistamines. "At the time of that attack," Sandy says, "my body was in a weakened condition because of the tetracycline I had ingested weeks before. The drug had apparently lodged in my liver and kidneys and was continuing to seep out. My body's supply of antihistamine was nearly depleted, which is why the (diet soda) incident nearly cost me my life.

"If nothing else, my ordeal taught me that I had affected an environment that allowed me to get into this condition," she says. She found that nothing the doctors could do was of any help. She was on her own. "Through reading, research, and practical application, I discovered that a diet that was as pure as possible, free of additives or chemicals of any kind, was my best defense. It allowed my body to function properly without having to work overtime to rid itself of toxins."

Sandy also discovered in the course of her research that she was not unique. She was not some kind of genetic mutant, but one of many who suffer from similar conditions. When she tried to buy the kinds of pure foods she needed to regain and keep her health, however, she found it a very difficult task. Even in health store foods, chemical additives are common. And the idea that produce is pure because it hasn't been processed doesn't hold true, either, she says. "For instance, a variety of vegetables and fruits, such as many of the tomatoes and bananas found in supermarkets, are picked when they're still green. Then they're gassed to make them ripen and change color." Residue from such gasses can bother sensitive people like Sandy and their effect on the rest of the population is questionable as well.

Shopping for food and cooking it threatened to become a full-time job for Sandy. She was becoming an expert in nutrition and cooking for an additive-free diet, however, and thought she'd like to combine use of her new knowledge with making it easier for people to buy natural foods. So the idea for her very own grocery store—one that would stock only foods that people with problems like hers could eat—was born. She was convinced, too, that even people without food allergies, people who were simply concerned about what they put into their bodies, would shop there as well.

At first, Sandy thought of having a small shop with just basic foods, but when she found a store site that seemed perfect, it would accommodate a much larger place. "The site that we picked was pure luck," she says. "A friend of mine lived nearby and knew the store that was in it was going out of business." A man had started a grocery store there with a $10,000 small business loan. "It was filthy and going broke. There was a separate meat market located in the store, but, luckily, it featured natural meats, so I thought we'd be a perfect combination."

Sandy decided to leave her 17-year teaching career and go into the food business. She knew little about the business world, however, so she combined her talents with those of Dan Vollard, who had had experience as manager of a health food store. "I thought I could use my nutrition knowledge and do the lecturing and public relations," Sandy says, "and that Dan could handle the business side of things." Sandy and Dan leased their first store, located in the Mar Vista section of Los Angeles, and began remodeling it. "My husband and I made the original investment of $90,000, which was cash we had," she says. That money paid for the remodeling and the initial stock. Although Sandy is now divorced, she admits that "I couldn't have done this without my husband's income to support us while we got off the ground. I made no money for myself the first two years." Any extra money Mrs. Gooch's earned during that time was reinvested in the store.

In planning the new store, Sandy says she was adamant

about not deviating from her natural foods standards, even though "my suppliers told me we couldn't make it with so narrow a philosophy. They asked me to put in a few items that weren't pure, but I felt I had to say no." She even refused to carry turbinado (partially refined) sugar or brown sugar because they are refined products.

Sandy and Dan used those suppliers, however, to educate themselves about the products that were available. And they asked for an analysis of what each product contained to determine that there were no hidden chemicals or additives not listed on the labels. Eventually, they found enough products and a large enough variety to stock their store.

Since they had a full 5000 square feet of space in their Mar Vista store, they also decided to expand the concept of the ordinary health food store. Sandy decided to open what she calls a mini-supermarket. That means that customers can buy more than food at Mrs. Gooch's. They can buy such essentials as facial tissue and tin foil as well. That way, Sandy feels, Mrs. Gooch's can be a one-stop store; her customers need never visit a supermarket or think of a trip to her store as an extra shopping trip.

The decor of Mrs. Gooch's Natural Food Store helps promote the return-to-nature philosophy of the store. Floors and counters are made of unpainted wood. And even display signs are framed in natural wood. Many products are sold from covered bins as they were in the old general store; customers scoop as much macaroni, walnuts, apple-cinnamon granola, dried apricots as they need and buy by weight.

The meat market is located at the back of the store and is a separate concession. Vic and Ken's Meats features beef raised without hormones or antibiotics and naturally raised poultry and pork. Meat prices are comparable with butcher shops, though somewhat higher than their supermarket counterparts. Again, customers ask the butchers (several of whom are women) to wrap as much of a certain meat as they can use. Vic and Ken's benefits from customers drawn to Mrs. Gooch's and vice versa.

The produce section displays a large variety of organically grown fruits and vegetables: apples, oranges, raspberries, pineapples, jicama, green beans, broccoli, and dozens more. Customers buy as much or as little as they want here, too, even things like alfalfa sprouts; nothing is pre-packaged. And produce prices are competitive with those at local supermarkets.

Sandy also packages her own line of natural vitamins and the selection is so large that the bottles line both sides of an aisle. Dan points out that he thinks the store's strict purity standards have made the sale of their vitamins particularly strong.

Also offered are several lines of natural cosmetics and such hard-to-find items as toothpaste and mouthwash that are totally free of chemical additives.

Sandy Gooch well realizes the necessity of giving food advice to customers in a store as specialized as Mrs. Gooch's, so she has hired a nutritionist to answer customer's questions when she's not around. Her sales staff is trained, too, in the latest research about vitamins and food purity. Sandy also keeps herself busy, in part, by conducting tours of the store and speaking on nutrition to interested groups. During the school year, it's common to enter Mrs. Gooch's and find a troop of seven- and eight-year-old schoolchildren learning about healthy eating at the store and being treated to a honey-sweetened yogurt cone on their way out. Sandy is still making good use of her teaching skills in promoting good nutrition and is gaining new customers for her store at the same time.

Mrs. Gooch's also has a gift section, featuring small appliances for food preparation, books on nutrition and cooking, plants, and handicrafts. One item that sells especially well here is really a store advertisement: a child-sized T-shirt that has the store's name and logo one one side and the slogan, "If you love me, don't feed me junk," on the other.

The store is branching out its private labels, too. In addition to vitamins, Sandy is putting the Mrs. Gooch's label on packaged granola, nuts, dried fruits, and other products with the ultimate goal of merchandising them to other health food stores around the country.

Her first two years in business were nearly impossible, Sandy admits, not because the store was unsuccessful, but because it was almost *too* successful. "We were very under-capitalized," she says, despite the decision to put off certain store improvements until the cash was in hand. For instance, she and Dan waited until the store was well established before installing a $13,000 floor. "Ironically, we had trouble because of our fantastic growth," she says. "We kept having to buy more freezers, desks, rent more office space. We needed more space to store things." In the room she uses for an office, boxes of canned and bottled goods are piled from floor to ceiling. Products move off her shelves so fast that a vast storage area is needed just to keep enough stock to satisfy the customers.

After the Mar Vista Mrs. Gooch's had been open for less than a year, Dan and Sandy decided to open a second store in the beachside community of Hermosa Beach. In July, 1977, they found a store there that was shaped like a barn and had previously housed a supermarket. Hermosa Beach is an upper-middle-class neighborhood where people tend to be both educated and aware of health concerns. It was a perfect location for the second Mrs. Gooch's. Dan Vollard now says that they probably were not as ready for expansion as they could have been when they opened that second site, but the opportunity was right, so they took it. The Hermosa Beach store features 6000 square feet, 3000 of which are used as a selling area. They remodeled once again, so the store's decor became much like that of the first Mrs. Gooch's, and spent $55,000 on their opening inventory. In October, 1977, the second store was in business.

In 1978, when Mrs. Gooch's had been in business a full two years, Dan Vollard invested $10,000 and became a full partner with Sandy Gooch. "We were trading our cash for his experience," Sandy says, explaining their unequal financial investments. She still feels she made an excellent trade.

Those first two years were difficult not only because Sandy

started two new stores, but they were also hard personally. She was not yet taking any money out of the business, so she was worried about finances. Her marriage was having problems, too. "My husband's business, an arts-and-crafts store, was declining while mine was taking off. I also think that my joy in working in my business and the fact that I was constantly being exposed to new philosophies and ways of life got between us." Her husband also had some definite ideas about how Mrs. Gooch's Natural Food Store should be run, and they were often different from Sandy's ideas. "He wanted to make money and I wanted to do the store more out of a dedication to my cause. It literally tore us apart. For instance, I refused to carry raw sugar, even in the back room. I felt we had to stick to our principles. On something like that, Ed would want to carry it because we could make more money. He felt I was naive and didn't know how to run the business to make the most money." Fortunately for Mrs. Gooch's, Sandy's insistence paid off. She now hears many customers saying how much they appreciate finding a food store they can really trust.

The Goochs' marriage broke up in 1979, and Sandy was on her own. That was a brutal year for her. "My father had just died of cancer and my mother, who is blind and deaf, found out she had leukemia. Then, when her father left, my daughter fell apart. She began having trouble in school and she's got a very high IQ." For a time, Sandy says she "thought of chucking the whole thing and devoting my time to my daughter. I dreaded coming back into the store because of all the memories and the fact that the store had done so much to break up my marriage." Soon those feelings passed, however, and Sandy began to realize that she needed the store to support herself, her daughter, and her disabled mother. By then, she was taking a salary of $2000 a month from the stores so she was able to meet her increased financial demands. She pays support for her mother, her home mortgage, and special tutoring and therapy charges for her daughter, as well as the usual living expenses.

"The store is all I have now," she says. "I can't go back to teaching because there are more teachers than jobs. And I have everything invested in this emotionally. As I look back, I can see it was either sink or swim." Sandy also visibly enjoys what she's doing. She's very good at proselytizing her pure-food nutrition ideas and she loves the feeling of success she's enjoyed with her stores.

Now that the business is several years old, the personal demands on Sandy have eased somewhat. She's no longer working 14-hour days as a rule, and she takes weekends off even though the stores are open seven days a week. She also has found a young woman to live with her and her daughter, thus taking some of the pressures of mothering off Sandy's shoulders. Things are settling down for her again.

Despite the personal traumas that accompanied her first few years as a food store owner, however, Sandy Gooch says there's really nothing she'd rather be doing today than running her business. She's very proud of the fact that people wanting to start similar stores in other parts of the country visit hers for ideas and assistance. And she's also proud of the recognition her success has brought to the idea of eating only pure foods. "It's given me a great deal of strength to do this and I know now that I can make it on my own," she says. Actually, Sandy is doing more than just surviving on her own. She's expanding her business and her cause at the same time.

Mrs. Gooch's Natural Food Store is just one kind of food store you might consider, of course. There are dozens of different ones that might be viable for you, depending on where you live, your local competition, your cooking interests, and so forth.

Perhaps you might like to run a store like the Tudor House British Center in Santa Monica, California. This charming shop features a variety of British foods: teas, jams, baked goods, sausages that British expatriates dearly miss and Americans love to sample. Some of the shop's appeal is that customers find food items there that they can't find elsewhere, of course. But much of it also is in the charm of the place, which couples the food shop with a real British tearoom where freshly baked scones and crumpets are available to munch while sipping tea that's definitely not brewed from a bag.

Or perhaps you'd prefer to own a shop like the French-influenced Pioneer Boulangerie, also located in Santa Monica. Pioneer began as a bakery, where possibly the best sour-dough French bread south of San Francisco is baked daily by a Basque family and their employees. Like Topsy, it grew, until it included a cafeteria that features mainly fresh breads and homemade soups, a gift shop, and a food store.

The food store, of course, could stand alone. Sold there are what might best be called a combination of baked goods and gourmet foods. The shop has a wide selection of wines, both French and Californian; exotic cheeses; jams, jellies and candies; and take-out deli-type foods. Also featured at Pioneer are a variety of coffee beans that can be ground on the site, if the customer wishes, plus a good selection of teas.

The atmosphere at Pioneer Boulangerie, which seems to be constantly expanding to accommodate the crowds it draws, is definitely European. Freshly baked rolls are sold from wooden bins and loaves of bread from wrought-iron baker's racks. The floors are wooden and the walls covered with maps of France and photographs of bakers. There is a glassed-in area that allows customers to watch white-hatted bakers at work baking French breads in real brick ovens. The saleswomen dress in French peasant dresses and crisp aprons. Half-timbering decorates the exterior of the building. And there are tables and chairs set around an outdoor patio so that people who purchase deli foods can eat them there, enjoying a sidewalk-café atmosphere.

The owners of Mrs. Gooch's Natural Food Store, the Tudor House British Center and Pioneer Boulangerie all had excellent ideas for food stores, ones that the public took to quickly. Your idea must be equally good. It must be something truly special if it's to succeed as these shops have. Ask yourself what's different about your proposed shop. Why will people want what you have to sell? What do you plan to offer that's not available in the local supermarket? Remember that you're asking your busy customers to make an extra shopping stop to patronize your store. They will need a good reason to justify that.

Sandy Gooch cites location as one of the primary concerns of a successful food store. She says her Mar Vista location was sheer luck. If it was, it was inspired luck. That section of Los Angeles is within five miles of both the extreme wealth of Bel Air and Beverly Hills, and the "nature child" feeling of parts of Ocean Park and Venice. The wealthy can afford to pay slightly higher prices and are interested in health and nutrition as well. The "nature child" customers Mrs. Gooch's attracts are strong believers in the pure food philosophy of life and, although they tend not to be affluent, they will spend a larger portion of their income on food if it means eating only organic vegetables and meat without DES, and having an opportunity to grind their own flour. At the same time, rents in Mar Vista are not high for the Los Angeles area. It was a perfect choice.

Sandy and partner Dan Vollard carefully inspected their second location, in Hermosa Beach, before they committed themselves to a lease. By then, they realized that the people living nearby had to be the kind who would be excited to have a supply of natural foods available to them. They could not survive merely by being closer to customers than the Safeway or being open longer hours than the 7-Eleven. They were offering a very special kind of food. In the wrong neighborhood they would fail.

The Tudor House British Center is located on the edge of a high-density apartment area in an affluent section of Santa Monica. Both the neighborhood's residents and the shop's patrons tend to be middle-aged and older. The tearoom on most afternoons is filled with blue-haired matrons enjoying the social atmosphere as much as the food available there.

In a neighborhood filled with young people, the Tudor House may well have been either less successful or an outright failure. Even in a predominantly non-white neighborhood, British products would undoubtedly not sell well. It, too, is in a good location.

A few customers may come from great distances if your shop is special enough. Sandy Gooch and Dan Vollard claim that some of their customers have travelled as far as 75 miles to patronize Mrs. Gooch's. Those customers are valued, of course, but they are also rare. And you may not be so lucky with your establishment. So be careful when you choose a location. It's vitally important.

Sandy also says that, with a food store, it's essential that you obtain a long lease—at least 10 years—when you choose a site. (Make sure to go over the lease with your lawyer; you want to have a way out if things don't work for any reason.) Location is such an important part of your establishment that you can't afford to have to move in a few years and re-establish yourself.

Consider carefully, too, how much space you'll need to run your business correctly and comfortably. The sales floor is one thing, but don't forget that you'll need some office space and possibly a great deal of storage space as well, depending upon the kind of store you plan. Sandy Gooch ended up moving her offices and some of her storage space into another small store a few feet away from her Mar Vista store. She was lucky to have the option, one you might not have if you lease too small a site. When she planned her Hermosa Beach store, she set aside half of the 6000 square feet of space there for storage and office space.

With a ten year or longer lease, and location such an important part of your shop's identity, moving to a larger location won't be feasible for you. And, if you lease too large a space, you'll be paying unnecessary rent and your excess space may even work against you. It could make your shop look sparsely stocked and poorly patronized, thus contributing to its failure, not its success. So choose your store's size as carefully as you select its location.

You'll need a staff of employees for your food store, something that's not true of all food businesses. You can teach cooking, write cookbooks, cater small parties, maybe even run a tiny bakery all by yourself. But there's no way you can run a food store by yourself. You'll need both help to stock your shelves and cashiers, at a minimum, even for a small store. Food stores are open longer hours than many food businesses, so it will be physically impossible for you to do everything yourself all the time.

Even with help, Mrs. Gooch's started with Sandy, Dan, and one other person, and now employs more than 90 people. Plan on putting in long hours at first. When she first opened, Sandy Gooch says she worked 14 hours a day, seven days a week, an exhausting schedule by any standards.

The kind of help you hire can contribute greatly to your store's image, so consider your applicants carefully. Sandy Gooch's help all look terrifically healthy and vibrant. Most are reasonably young, and they have glowing complexions and slender bodies. Consider for a moment what hiring an overweight cashier suffering from a bad case of acne would do to the store's health-foods image. It's important, too, that Sandy's employees agree with her philosophy; not that they'll be fired for eating a candy bar, but that they can preach healthy eating from their own convictions and that they stay informed about new information on natural foods.

The saleswomen at Pioneer Boulangerie are all dressed in French outfits, helping to create the feeling that, for a few moments, the customer has been transported to France.

And the staff at Tudor House British Center are all British. Their delightful accents carry the ring of conviction as they advise customers how to prepare bangers and mash or a traditional yule log for the holidays. They're mainly middle-aged women, too, like most of Tudor House's customers.

You will also undoubtedly need financial and legal assistance for your food store, and these people should be chosen with as much care as you would choose them for any other business.

When it comes to choosing sources from which to buy

your store's stock, help is available from a variety of areas. The Small Business Administration can be particularly beneficial. For example, the SBA's Service Corps of Retired Executives (SCORE) will readily give you the name of a retired person who has run a small store like yours; his or her advice about suppliers and other matters can be invaluable. You may also be able to get advice from other store owners in your community. And a third source is the Yellow Pages of your phone book. Look under the listing, "Food Brokers."

You may have to use some trial and error with your suppliers. Check prices, of course, but also be aware of how quality compares from one supplier to another, which ones deliver, and which ones deliver on time. Don't be afraid to switch allegiance if price, quality or service are not right for your enterprise.

Carefully consider exactly what products you'll sell. Sandy Gooch recommends letting your suppliers give you advice on this. They know what's available, what's sold well or poorly in other neighborhoods. Listen to them, but make your own decisions in the end. Although Sandy gained some valuable advice from her suppliers, she also discounted some of what they had to say. When they suggested she would fail unless she expanded her selection to include certain products she considered impure, for instance, she didn't listen. Sometimes that meant that a certain kind of product was not available in her store (she couldn't find margarine without chemicals, for example, so she didn't carry margarine at all), but she felt her store's integrity was more important. Decide where you stand on the kind of products you want to carry, get advice, and, like Sandy, make your own decision.

How many different products you carry is an important business decision. If you have a coffee and tea shop, for instance, how many varieties should you stock? If you have too few, it won't be worth a customer's time to patronize your shop. But if you have too many, you may find that some become stale before you can sell them and that customers become confused by the number of choices you present.

Consider, too, whether you'll carry any products other than foods in your shop. Sandy Gooch carries green plants, cosmetics, a line of gift items (many of them with bows already attached), books on nutrition and cooking, and small food-preparation gadgets such as vegetable steamers. People drawn to her store by the foods often find themselves spending additional money on these attractively displayed items.

The Pioneer Boulangerie has an entire gift shop upstairs, featuring items that are food-related, but also things selected with an eye toward the unusual: wine glasses, gourmet bakeware, coffee grinders, handmade potholders, and aprons. And the Tudor House British Center carries even nonfood-related items from the British Isles, such as neckties in a variety of Scottish clan plaids.

The right additions to your product line can greatly increase your shop's income, and they have the added advantage, unlike food, of not spoiling. If that cheese board and knife you carry in your wine and cheese shop doesn't sell for awhile, the worst thing that will happen is that you will have some capital tied up. Unlike cheese that doesn't sell, the board and knife won't end up in the garbage can.

Both your staff and the stock you carry will help create your store's image. And, in a specialty store, image is highly important. Sandy Gooch has very carefully designed her stores' image and she enhances it with decor, her staffing, the food and non-food items she sells, and her advertising. Mrs. Gooch's has a back-to-nature feeling about it that's carefully planned and cultivated. It's reminiscent of the old general store and makes customers feel that they're back in the good old days when things were simpler, foods were pure, and they could trust their shopkeepers.

Sandy tends to details, too. For example, she occasionally publishes a newsletter, *The Gazette*, that's packed in customers' grocery bags. It's printed in sepia tones (brown ink on beige paper), again creating the impression of something aged, and features recipes, health information, and promotion articles on the store. Even those grocery bags are specially printed in a brown overall design that carries out the store's image. The store's logo incorporates its name, Mrs. Gooch's Natural Food Stores, with characters that look as though they were lifted from an old Mother Goose reader. The characters include a sheep and a pig, completely clothed and engaged in a conversation; a boy and girl dressed in old-fashioned clothing; and a goose wearing an apron and bonnet and nibbling on an ear of corn.

Sandy Gooch believes it's important to spend money creating an image, because the right image draws customers and results in increased sales. She and Dan spent 10 percent of their expected gross sales receipts on advertising when they opened the Hermosa Beach store. Dan Vollard explains that there's nothing worse than a big new store with only a few customers in it. "Although we usually don't overemphasize any one department, we stocked a lot of perishables, to look good," he said of the Hermosa Beach opening. Buying only a few of each kind of vegetable and fruit might appear to customers that the store expected a small turnout. "We needed good traffic to move the produce out, rather than lose money on what didn't sell and had to be discarded."

They hired an advertising agency, which analyzed the local news media and surveyed market data; it was finally decided to spend the entire advertising budget in two local newspapers.

The kind of ads Mrs. Gooch's runs are as much image ads as product ads. Often a full page in size, they explain the store's philosophy. The first one told Sandy Gooch's personal story: how she created her store after her almost fatal reaction to various food additives. The ads also often mention a few specials (perhaps a sale on honey, bulk rice, or oranges), but the reader is left more with an impression of the store than with a list of bargains. The ads for Mrs. Gooch's recognize that a health food store offers a special service more than a bargain price, so they're very different from the ones run by the typical supermarket.

If you decide that advertising is necessary to promote your

store, consider hiring an agency. The money a good one saves you in mistakes not made can be substantial.

Once you're well established as a specialty store, advertising will become less necessary. Because your business doesn't depend on your tomatoes being five cents a pound cheaper than the ones sold by your competitors, your customers will return simply because you're there and you give them what they want. If someone wants jasmine tea or a special blend of coffee and you have the only coffee and tea store in the area, you'll get the business. *If*, that is, the customer knows you exist. So the inclusion of advertising in your financial budget is most important during that first year or two, while you're building your clientele.

Being savvy about public relations is important, too. Sandy Gooch's lectures, stints on radio talk shows, and tours for schoolchildren are all excellent PR vehicles. They help create her store's image and gain her more customers at the same time. Sandy recommends carefully planning events to promote your store. For example, "make your opening exciting," she says. "Give away samples and prizes, welcome customers and listen to what they say they want." An event like this can cost you some money, but it may be less than what you'd spend on a paid advertising campaign. Another important and helpful public relations event that Sandy has run is a baking contest where all ingredients in the baked goods must be natural. Fundraising bake sales with natural products have been held for schools and charities as well. And some local elementary schools have incorporated Sandy's talks into their nutrition programs. Children learn about good eating habits this way and later they often make posters promoting good nutrition habits or write letters to Sandy expressing their gratitude for her help in teaching them about food. Such posters and letters often become part of the decor at Mrs. Gooch's, and needless to say, when these children go home, they tell their parents about Mrs. Gooch's and help Sandy and Dan gain more customers.

Shopping in a speciality food store should be *fun*, Sandy Gooch believes, and use of special events that involve the customer help create that atmosphere. If shopping in your store is enjoyable and entertaining, customers will come back again and again. So remember that what you sell is only part of what's important in running a specialty food store.

Before you open a store of your own, Sandy advises that you study similar stores and learn from them. "The best way to do that is to get a job in a store like the one you want to open," she says. "Work there, even if it's for minimum wage. You'll see what it's like and what the customers want." If that's not feasible, visit similar stores even if they're located some distances from your home. In fact, if they're *not* located a good distance away, you're probably choosing the wrong location for your store.

As with all food businesses, adequate financing is vital. You will need enough money to lease your store, remodel it, hire staff, stock your shelves, and pay for initial advertising and public relations campaigns. This is one of the most expensive food businesses to start. Remember that it's going to take you some time to gather a loyal clientele and that in the beginning you're going to be in the red. With Mrs. Gooch's Hermosa Beach store, it was three months before the store began to earn money, and that may be some kind of record. You may have to plan on six months or even a year, particularly in a business where unsold merchandise may well mean discarded merchandise. Undoubtedly, too, you'll experience some trial and error in the products you buy. You may stock your cheese store with special Danish cheeses, for instance, only to find that no one wants them. Your customers may lean toward Wisconsin cheeses and be unwilling to pay a higher price for the imported kind. The second time around, you can order more from Wisconsin and less from Denmark, but in the meantime, you're stuck with Danish cheeses that aren't selling. If you don't have the capital to withstand this kind of mistake, your business is in trouble. So plan ahead and get the best financial advice available before you take the plunge with your own food store business.

If you have a good idea for a food store that grows out of your cooking interests, you can make a go of it today despite the success of supermarkets and convenience food stores. Just make sure that your idea is for something *special:* something people can't find at these more common establishments, and something enough people want so that you'll be financially successful.

Pay attention to your store's location, its staffing, the products you'll carry, and its image as well, and you may find yourself the proprietor of an establishment just as successful as Mrs. Gooch's Natural Food Store, Tudor House British Center, or Pioneer Boulangerie. There's still room today for many more specialty food stores. Maybe one of them will be yours.

6

Your Restaurant Venture

When good cooks think of opening their own businesses, a restaurant is often the first kind that comes to mind. Each year, some 10,000 home chefs open their own small restaurants. Perhaps you dream of being one of these chefs. It can be very rewarding, both financially and in terms of ego gratification. But it's also one of the most expensive and risky food-related businesses to run.

The financial investment needed to start a restaurant is often as high as opening your own food store. You probably will find yourself working 14 hours a day, six days a week, at least at first. And your chances of failure in the first year are one in three.

But Americans still go out to eat; their restaurant expenditures go up every year. Eating out, of course, provides more than nourishment for the body. It's also recreational, a chance to relax and enjoy life. If you become a chef in your own restaurant, you become the host to people who want more than good food; they also want an enjoyable atmosphere, a certain kind of personality in a restaurant.

If you can offer these things, withstand a pace that some restaurant owners have described as killing, and are unafraid to take risks, you could become one of the two in three new restauranteurs who succeeds. You'll probably earn, on the average, between $20,000 and $40,000 a year. You'll have the satisfaction of being your own boss. And you may come to enjoy local celebrity status as well.

Charles Baron of San Clemente, California, is a classic example of an excellent amateur cook who took his friends' advice and opened his own restaurant. Charles has always loved to cook and had become very accomplished, although, "I never had any formal training in cooking," he says. He'd been in the menswear business for 20 years, then retired from that and became a portrait artist for another 14 years.

"I was retired again and looking for something to do," he says. Friends were impressed with the six-course dinners he would prepare for them at home when he and his wife, Jacqueline, entertained. Why not make that "something to do" a small restaurant, they urged?

Charles had "less than $50,000" to invest when he began to look at available sites. Newport Beach, where Charles had worked as a portrait artist and where the Barons lived, was out; rents were too high there. So he searched the surrounding area and settled on a place three blocks from the ocean in less affluent San Clemente. "It had been a hamburger place on one side and a steak-and-potatoes place on the other. And they shared a joint kitchen," he recalls. "I was looking for something that looked like a restaurant on the outside, so that I wouldn't have the expense of remodeling the facade, too."

Charles and Jacqueline had the entire inside of the building gutted and they designed what they wanted for their dream restaurant, Bonsoir Charles. "My wife would say, 'We need this' and 'We need that' and we'd get it," Charles recalls. It took shape gradually. Together, and with professional construction help, the Barons spent about two months remodeling their restaurant.

They took particular care in planning the atmosphere of Bonsoir Charles, while keeping the costs down as much as possible. For example, they stitched their tablecloths out of bedsheets to save money, but they gained a most interesting look at the same time. The color scheme is apricot and green. "We use a dark green table liner and light apricot tablecloth," says Charles. The walls are a latticework of apricot against a dark green background. Elegance is the effect Charles and Jacqueline wanted to achieve. When they opened, in May, 1975, they used real bone china ("not restaurant china"), genuine silverware, and crystal glassware. Today, the silverware and crystal are gone—"We began losing too much of it," Charles says—but the bone china remains. "There is a lot of breakage, but we feel that's part of the cost of doing business. We really enjoy it when our guests turn over a plate to see who makes the china."

Charles decided on a fixed-price menu. Bonsoir Charles offers a choice of four to five different entrees every evening around which a six-course meal is planned. "We offer one or two meat entrees, a fish entree and one or two fowl entrees each evening." Charles serves as both chef and maitre d' and Jacqueline is both pastry chef and hostess.

Courses included in the set price of $12.95 include an appetizer, soup, pasta, a relieving course, the entree, and salad. Drinks and dessert are extra, and the average party spends about $22 per person for an evening at Bonsoir Charles. The cuisine is classic French and Charles himself recites the oral menu to each party. "Many of our guests don't really know classic French cooking," he says, "so I explain to them how each dish is made."

He feels that one reason for the success of Bonsoir Charles is the "one-to-one relationship I have with the guest." People like that personal touch. "After all, in the restaurant business, you sell more than food to the guest. You sell him the personality of the place, too."

Charles is able to serve as both chef and maitre d' because he uses his time very carefully. He does all the food shopping himself, too, setting aside time each day. "If I have to go to San Diego or Los Angeles for an item I want, I'll do it," he says. Since the restaurant is open only four nights a week (Wednesday through Saturday), he has three other days for a lengthy shopping trip if one is necessary. During the day, he cooks, partially preparing most dishes. And, in the evening, while he dons his maitre d' hat and chats with the customers, his two assembly chefs put together the meals as they are ordered. "The only thing we don't prepare partially in advance," Charles says, "is a dish that is flambéed at the table, like Steak Diane."

Bonsoir Charles' four-day schedule is new. "In the beginning we were open seven days a week," Charles says, "and that was a killing pace. Then we cut back to six days and it was still a killing pace. We tried five days for awhile, and that was successful. But our customers are generous; we found that we can do more business being open four days than five. And that way we have three days to do other things." Bonsoir Charles is available for special parties on the days it's closed to the public, so Charles and Jacqueline don't always spend those days away from work. Often they find themselves hosts to weddings, anniversary parties, and other special events.

"Our restaurant is generally filled, although there are ups and downs in this business," Charles says. Summer is a busy season for Bonsoir Charles, as it is for all businesses in San Clemente. But, "if there's some big production on television, we feel it. People stay home." The place seats 46 comfortably. "We give guests plenty of elbow room. There has to be room for our serving carts between tables, so the spacing is quite comfortable."

Space in the kitchen is much more at a premium and the kitchen design is the one thing Charles would change if he had the opportunity to do things over again. "I would design it to make the line flow easier." The kitchen is approximately 9 by 18 feet and "it really gets crowded when the waiters, the busboy, the assembly chefs, my wife, and I are all in there." He advises others thinking about opening a restaurant to plan carefully how a dish will get from the chef to the waiter and make that process as logical and easy as possible. "Think about how you're going to get the portions out. What if you have a table of 20? How are you going to get them all served before things get cold?"

The Barons decided to serve only wine and beer at Bonsoir Charles, for largely financial reasons. "It was relatively easy to get a wine and beer license. We just went to the ABC (Alcoholic Beverage Commission), applied for the license, paid the fee, and got it. A full bar would have been too expensive. I think a liquor license at the time would have cost me about $40,000, and I couldn't see investing that much money in something when I didn't know whether or not it was going to work out. That was too much jeopardy." Charles feels he hasn't lost customers because his place doesn't serve hard liquor, however. He sees his diners as sophisticated types who appreciate good food and fine wine, not as hard drinkers.

Serving six courses to every patron was an ambitious plan, they soon found out. "For each course you add," Charles says, "your work load seems to go up about four times, not just once. You need to have excellent timing." He adds that most restaurants serve only two courses, the salad or soup, and the entree. He and Jacqueline felt they needed some practice before they opened their restaurant, so they invited their friends to dine and practiced on them. Eventually, they and their staff got it right. They could serve all six courses on time and at the right temperature.

The menu at Bonsoir Charles changes every night and Charles tries to repeat dishes as infrequently as possible. "I devour cookbooks and I dream about new dishes all the time," he says. One of the biggest joys in running his own restaurant is to try a new dish and then have the pleasure of watching his guests' enjoyment in eating it.

While running a restaurant can be personally rewarding, it also has to make money to exist. Charles Baron refuses to discuss specific financial figures, but a recent article on Bonsoir Charles in the *Los Angeles Times* included a financial projection by one of the *Times'* business writers and it seems quite accurate. That projection said that the restaurant earned a gross revenue of $175,000 a year for 1980 and that the Barons' net on that amount was approximately 20 percent, or $35,000.

Charles does point out that his is a low-labor business. Since both he and his wife wear two hats, they're able to keep labor costs to a minimum and, he says, "that's the secret of our success financially." His other employees include two waiters and a busboy, who work for minimum wage and gratuities; the two assembly chefs; and clean-up help. "The dishwasher is particularly important here," he says, "because every guest uses about seven dishes." There's all that very breakable china to consider, too.

When Bonsoir Charles opened, the price for dinner was only $7.50. The raise to $12.95 reflects both six years of inflation and the Barons' initial trouble deciding on a price that was profitable. "The first year was the most difficult," Charles says, "because we had to learn about things like pricing." Today, not all the meals cost the same to prepare, but they average out to a nice profit. "Sometimes the fish or meat courses may cost more than the fowl course, particularly if we're serving breast of chicken. But other times, if we serve duckling, pheasant, or quail, the fowl course may be the highest." Charles has learned how to balance his costs for each evening so that he earns an income from his business. Statistically, 50 percent of the customers order meat, 25 percent fish, and 25 percent fowl.

Charles will also prepare special-order dishes with advance notice. An example is a special pressed duck that requires a half-hour ceremony at the table. For that, he adds a $4.00 surcharge.

The $12.95 fixed price seems quite reasonable by big-city standards, although Charles points out that his place is considered to be rather high-priced by San Clemente standards. The location of a restaurant can determine its prices as much as the food it serves. "If we were located in Beverly Hills," Charles points out, "we could charge from $25 to $35 for the same menu." Still, he is happy with his location for now and would not want to move to Beverly Hills, where his rent would also be astronomically higher. "Someday I might like to have a place in Newport Beach, but I don't want to have two restaurants. Then I'd lose the one-on-one with my customers and the pleasure would be gone."

Although Charles believes, "Running a restaurant is much harder work than either the menswear business or portrait painting," it's work he loves. "When we get recognition, like an article in the *Los Angeles Times,* or a good restaurant review, it's a real ego builder. When you think of rewards, a good article is a big one." Bonsoir Charles has had several of those. During its first year in business, the Southern California Restaurant Writers Association selected Bonsoir Charles as the most promising new restaurant, an award that not only provided a great deal of ego gratification for Charles and Jacqueline, but increased their clientele as well.

Bonsoir Charles is also listed in at least three restaurant guides, Charles says. And it's been well reviewed not only in the *Times,* but the *Santa Ana Register* as well. Add this to word-of-mouth recommendations and business is good. "We haven't done any advertising until recently," he says. Everything helps.

After six years in business, Charles Baron still exhibits his original enthusiasm for his project, something he recommends that others be able to do if they're going to take on the job of running their own restaurants. "Put down on paper what your dream is," he recommends, "and analyze it. Let it sit for two or three months. Is your enthusiasm still there? If not, you don't belong in this business."

Charles knows that he, too, should get out if his enthusiasm ever wanes. "We'll run this business just as long as we *enjoy* running it," he says.

And, right now, that promises to be a very long time.

Like Bonsoir Charles, Casa Monica in Santa Monica, California, is a husband-and-wife-owned restaurant started by an amateur chef. Owners Tom and Lynn Wagstaff, however, are really just starting out on their working lives. When they opened their restaurant in 1978, Tom was only 30 and Lynn only 23. And, unlike the Barons, the Wagstaffs see a second, or even a third, restaurant as a concrete possibility in their future.

"Tom had always wanted to have his own restaurant," says Lynn. "He used to cook when we entertained, especially big pots of spaghetti."

Tom recalls that his mother tried to teach him to cook when he was a boy, but he resisted. "I love to eat, though, and when I moved out on my own, I suffered through two or three months of frozen dinners and then I began to teach myself to cook." It became a primary love.

Tom also had a desire to have his own business, and he'd had two different ones before the restaurant. One was installing side moldings on cars and the other was selling decorative pub mirrors. Lynn was previously a legal secretary, model, and actress.

"We found this restaurant in the business opportunities ads of the newspaper," Lynn recalls. It was a failed Italian restaurant. The Wagstaffs had both worked and saved their money, bought MGM stock with their savings, and watched the stock rise in value. Then they decided to trade their stock for a business of their own. "We offered the owner a third less than he was asking and we never thought he'd take it," she says. "But the real estate agent called us the next day and told us our offer was accepted." The Wagstaffs won't discuss exactly how much they paid for Casa Monica, but they were able to buy it outright without bank financing. "We put in our money, my folks put in some, and we got a silent partner through a friend," Lynn says.

The next step was getting the place in shape. Lynn says that the kitchen was the worst project. "It took four of us two and a half weeks of cleaning to get off all the grease and get rid of the bugs. It was really awful." In fact, Lynn chided the health department official who later came to inspect their kitchen for not having done a better job with the previous owner. They remodeled the entire place, which is located in a small shopping center on the affluent north side of Santa Monica.

Like nearly all new business owners, Lynn and Tom wish they had a little more capital when they started. "For example," says Lynn, "my mother made our curtains from fabric we got at a discount. I would have liked to be able to choose exactly what we wanted, but we had to save money. We bought all our own dishes and glasses, too. We went to the Franciscan Shop and bought their overstock. Now we want to buy Cordon Bleu dishes as we can afford them."

The Wagstaffs also had to quit their jobs to open Casa Monica, a move that cost them $3000 a month in lost income. And for the six months it took before the restaurant began to show a profit, they lived largely on the overdraft protection of their checking account.

Like all restaurants, Casa Monica needed certain legal permits before Tom and Lynn could reopen it. And, unlike the Barons, the Wagstaffs found dealing with the Alcoholic Beverage Commission to be an ordeal. Tom says, "The real headache was the ABC. I think we must have gone there 30 times, largely because they don't explain things to you very well. We had to be fingerprinted and the whole bit." Like Bonsoir Charles, Casa Monica has only a beer and wine license.

"Having a beer and wine license means that you have to have both a men's and a ladies' room," says Lynn, so that meant remodeling. "And, if you have a 50-person capacity, you have to have two doors because of the fire regulations." Their place was inspected by both the fire department and the health department. An additional requirement was a business permit.

Opening night at Casa Monica was attended mainly by Tom and Lynn's friends. "We invited them to eat at half price so we could practice on them," Lynn says. She also recalls that opening night was "a real shock to think that all these people actually came and thought we could do this thing. We weren't so sure."

That first night saw the first of many menu changes as the

Wagstaffs employed trial and error in pricing and selections. "At first, we offered pizza," Lynn says, "but the second night I crossed it off all the menus. There just wasn't room to cook it. We used our double pizza ovens to bake breads and finally sold them. Also, pizza is a low-cost item that brings in families. If you have a lot of families, then people who want a higher quality food and are willing to pay for it don't come."

That first menu was underpriced, they learned. Their second menu broke about even and now they're making money. The menu has been changed six times since they opened, and four of those changes were drastic ones. Now, their featured dishes have become much more sophisticated than that original pizza. Some of their best-sellers include Fettucine Casa Monica (spinach pasta in cream sauce with mushrooms, onions, proscuitto, and chicken), Fusilli Carbonara (noodles with eggs, bacon, Parmesan cheese, whipping cream, chili peppers, and parsley), Veal de la Casa (veal with two cream sauces, shallots, ham, and fontina cheese), and Chicken Sorrentino (boneless breast of chicken in a sherry sauce with eggplant, proscuitto, mushrooms, and mozzarella cheese). They also offer fresh fish every night and six to eight specials, in addition to the dishes listed on the menu. While the original menu offered complete dinners, now everything is a la carte.

Since they opened, Tom, who serves as chef, has honed his cooking skills, both through practice and through cooking lessons with Wolfgang Puck, the famous chef at Ma Maison. At first Lynn, too, did some of the cooking. But now they've hired a sous chef and Lynn serves as hostess and wine stewardess. They also employ two waitresses and a dishwasher. "At first we paid the other cook $5.00 an hour," Lynn says, "and that seemed like a fortune to us." That wage has now been raised and the sous chef is left in charge of Casa Monica on Sundays and Mondays, when Tom and Lynn take their days off, and also for a week each year when they take a vacation. The waitresses and dishwasher are paid minimum wage. "Dishwashers are a dime a dozen," Lynn says, "but it's very hard to find one who will stay and do a good job."

Eventually, the Wagstaffs were able to buy out their silent partner and take in a friend as a partner. "We offered to buy out our silent partner once and he didn't like our offer," Tom says. "Then we made the same offer a year later and, by then, he needed the money for his law practice, so he took it. We figure we used his money at an interest rate of only 6.2 percent a year. That was much better than a bank would have charged us. Besides, we had no credit rating, so a bank probably wouldn't have lent to us."

Tom has a good sense of business, something they feel many chefs do not have. "So many are creative in the kitchen but know nothing about finances," says Lynn. Because of Tom's financial acumen, Casa Monica is becoming very successful. That change to the a la carte menu was one good decision. It has kept prices apparently low, but people tend to order more than just an entree, thus building a higher tab.

Casa Monica also caters only to parties of four or more. "We have only nine booths and three tables," says Lynn, "so there was too much waiting if we seated by couples. And people coming in groups tend more often to be on time and to spend more money." That has not cost them business. Tom says, "We're full on weekends now and we've had as much as an hour and a half wait."

Their income from Casa Monica is something the Wagstaffs won't discuss specifically, but Tom says that "we can live the way we want to now. We rent a house in Malibu and we have a boat and we're not really hurting." An estimate of Casa Monica's gross annual receipts would probably be about $200,000.

What accounts for the popularity of Casa Monica when so many other new restaurants fail? Lynn thinks it's succeeding because "we care about what we do. This is like coming to our house for dinner. We know many of the people we serve and everything is cooked to order. We use real butter and whipped cream and offer handmade desserts. There's just more of *us* in it."

Tom and Lynn's personalities and looks do make a difference. Young, blond, tanned and healthy-looking, they could be an advertisement for the California good life.

Perhaps because of their youth, the Wagstaffs seem un-aware of the risk they took in opening their own restaurant, particularly now that it's paid off. "I never considered our *not* making it," Lynn says. "I have always believed in the old saying: where there's a will there's a way. This is like being on a diet. The first part's the hardest and then it gets easier."

They do advise others thinking of their own restaurants to realize how much effort it takes, however. "Make sure this is the one thing you want to do in your life," Lynn says. "You give up your social life. Have a lot of friends who will help you out and don't be afraid to do all the jobs yourself."

Tom agrees. "We've both washed dishes here." And he adds, "Don't let others influence you too much. Do it your own way."

They also both feel that it's important for both husband and wife to be involved in the business together. That gives each of them someone close to talk to and share with. And, with the long hours a restaurant requires of its owners, that can be very important.

In the future, Tom and Lynn Wagstaff see either a second restaurant or a move to a larger place. And, five years down the road, they're thinking of selling out here and moving to Hawaii, where they dream of owning a restaurant on the beach at Kona. Getting out of the restaurant business is definitely not in their future plans, despite its demanding pace. "I have no regrets about the restaurant business," says Tom. "It's a little like being a movie star in a way. You're always in the limelight. People—and some of them are famous—come in and tell us they've always wanted to have a little restaurant of their own, but never were able to do it. They envy us."

As you can see from the stories of the Barons and the Wagstaffs, opening your own restaurant is no easy proce-dure. It entails long, hard hours, and, if necessary, being willing and able to do everything yourself: from being the chef to cleaning the bathroom; from greeting the guests to waiting on tables; from ordering supplies to finding financial backers who believe in your project enough to invest their money in it. But the rewards can be great, too, both financially and personally. If you haven't been discouraged by what you've read and still want to pursue your own dream of a restaurant, there are several things you must consider.

As with any other food business, ask yourself why your restaurant will be different. Why will customers patronize your place instead of the restaurants that already exist in your town? The answer may be as simple as your steak-and-potatoes place serving better steak and potatoes than the one down the road. Or it may mean that there is no Chinese eatery within 50 miles and you're planning to provide one. It could also mean that the personality of your restaurant—and personality means not only you and your staff, but the physical atmosphere, the ambiance of the place—is more charming, more romantic, more fun, than the competition.

The personality of your establishment can also include such variables as the hours you're open. Perhaps, like Charles and Jacqueline Baron, you'd like to have an elegant dinner house that's open only four nights a week. Or maybe, like Lynn and Tom Wagstaff, you'll opt for all seven. What about lunches? Will you be open for both lunch and dinner? You might even have in mind a place that would be open *only* for lunch, from Monday through Friday, if you locate in an office complex.

If you have a satisfactory answer to why people would patronize your dream, and you think you can be successful, think location next. Location can determine a dozen things about your restaurant: what prices you can charge; whether your competition will bury you; whether you can stay afloat financially while you establish your business; what kind of clientele you can hope to attract; whether your place should strive for a romantic atmosphere or maybe a funky, fun atmosphere; whether people can park nearby; the very success of your restaurant.

Both Bonsoir Charles and Casa Monica are located in buildings that were formerly other restaurants; this is by far the least expensive route to follow. If you can find an existing restaurant in a good location, you won't have to construct a new kitchen, the primary large expense in opening a restaurant.

Ask yourself why the former restaurant failed, however. Why do you expect to be successful in a location where someone else's dream died? Sometimes, as Lynn and Tom Wagstaff found, the previous owner just wasn't a very good restauranteur. As shown by his filthy kitchen, he didn't put as much of himself and his pride into the business as the Wagstaffs do. In the case of Bonsoir Charles, Charles and Jacqueline Baron changed the place from hamburgers and steaks to classic French cuisine and added a whole new look to the interior as well. For them, that was enough of a change to make the place successful even though it had not done well under the previous management.

Pay attention to the size of your building. How many customers a day must you serve to make a profit? If you specialize in a low-cost item, pizza, for instance, you will have to serve a great many people to make money. A restaurant that seats 25 isn't going to allow you to do that unless you're also running a large take-out service. If, however, you plan to specialize in intimate dinners with many special courses, don't go for a place that seats 200 unless you plan on hiring a huge staff and you also locate in a city where you have enough potential customers to make that idea feasible.

The economic bracket of the neighborhood in which you locate matters a great deal, too. If you plan to locate in a lower- or middle-income neighborhood, your customers are not going to patronize your place if a $35-per-person dinner tab is the norm there. On the other hand, if you're thinking of Beverly Hills, a hamburger joint isn't very feasible, if only because the high rents you'll have to pay there will force you to charge more than most people will pay for a hamburger. Remember Charles Baron's prediction that his six-course dinners could rise in price from $12.95 to as much as $35 if he relocated from San Clemente to Beverly Hills.

Location has a heavy hand in determining the prices you can charge.

The level of sophistication of the people who live nearby matters, too. A restaurant like Bonsoir Charles might not survive in a college town where pizza and hamburgers reign. On the other hand, a simple little spaghetti house might die in an area where dining out means being treated to exotic cuisine.

And, of course, it's obvious that such extras as a restaurant with a view can make a great deal of difference. A panoramic view of the Atlantic, for instance, might overcome a multitude of sins in the kitchen. People will eat even mediocre food happily if the view makes up for it.

As with any other food business, consider your competition before you decide upon a location. This doesn't necessarily mean avoiding an area with many other restaurants. La Cienega Boulevard in Los Angeles, for example, is known as "Restaurant Row" to locals, because it's home to dozens of restaurants. People go to La Cienega Boulevard and try one place one evening, another the next. Some restaurants there succeed wildly while others fail just as wildly.

The kind of competition to avoid is opening a restaurant specializing in roast beef across the street from Lawry's The Prime Rib, an internationally famous place that's known as the epitome of roast beef restaurants. If one restaurant seems to have cornered the market for a certain kind of food or atmosphere, try either another location or another idea.

When you find a building you think will work for you, pay particular attention to the size and design of the kitchen. Charles Baron says the one thing he would gladly change about Bonsoir Charles is the design of its kitchen. Remember that your entire staff may be in the kitchen at once during the top of the dinner hour. Will they trip over each other? If so, perhaps some remodeling is in order, or else finding another building may be necessary.

Look, too, at just how much remodeling will be necessary to make this into the restaurant of your dreams. If you're buying a lease on a failed Italian restaurant and plan to make it into a place offering continental Italian cuisine, as Lynn and Tom Wagstaff did, you can do a minimum of remodeling. If, on the other hand, you're looking at a building that was previously a dress shop, you've got your work cut out for you: new kitchen, new exterior, new everything.

Robert Patterson of Laventhol and Horwath, an accounting and consulting firm in Los Angeles that specializes in the restaurant business, says that your initial capital determines whether you buy an existing restaurant and maintain it pretty much as it is; redecorate an existing place to reflect another type of restaurant; or construct a new one. Unless you have a great deal of money to invest, you will want to lease instead of buy your real estate. Laventhol says a fair price for an existing restaurant is about four to five times the expected gross income. A major restaurant construction job can cost as much as $200 a square foot.

You will need to plan carefully just how much capital you will have available and how you will raise it. Charles Baron was lucky. He had enough of his own money to invest without additional help. You may not be so lucky. The Wagstaffs found a silent partner, that is, a person who invested money in their business with the hope of making a profit. Without him, they would have been unable to open. Robert Patterson says that particularly in today's economic climate, banks are *very* reluctant to invest in restaurants. They feel that restaurants are just too risky. So, if you don't have the personal funds necessary, try borrowing from friends and relatives or selling limited partnerships.

The amount of money you'll need to open your own restaurant can range from little to astronomical. You could probably use up a million-dollar investment to open a luxurious place on Manhattan's Upper East Side; or you could take over a small-town truck stop for a few hundred.

You'll need paper and a sharp pencil to figure out just how much you will need for your specific idea and location. Get sound financial advice and don't underestimate your monetary needs. One of the biggest reasons for a new restaurant's failure is that the owners didn't have enough capital to withstand the initial time period that it always takes to become established.

The level of financial success you can hope for also ranges greatly. On the downside, some diners earn their owners only a scrape-by income. And then there are the restaurant legends, like Ma Maison of Hollywood, the famous restaurant where the stars gather to be seen by other stars and the cuisine is known worldwide for its excellence. Ma Maison was begun with a $40,000 investment put up by eight backers (led by dancer Gene Kelly). In its first year, it almost died, but today it grosses $10,000 a day even though there are only 38 tables. Now that's financial success!

Patterson says that a typical net profit on a restaurant is about four percent of the gross income, or eight percent for a restaurant in California. Of course, if you handle much of the labor yourself, as the Barons and Wagstaffs do, you'll end up saving what you would pay someone else to do those jobs as well.

Before you sign the lease on that new building, get some good legal as well as financial help. You'll need a good attorney not only to help you with the lease itself, but to make sure you're in compliance with all the laws your town has that cover restaurants. The legal details you'll become involved with may include, for example, a business license, zoning regulations, meeting the fire code, a visit from the health department, and getting an alcoholic beverage license.

When you have your location established, your financing set, and you're sure you're in compliance with local laws, then you're ready to assemble your staff, another important part of your restaurant's personality. If you're planning to act as chef, who will fill in for you when you're ill or want a day off? Can you handle *all* the cooking yourself? If not, choose your kitchen help carefully. Many a restaurant's reputation has been ruined by sporadic food quality.

Consider carefully, too, the people you'll hire to meet the public. They help convey your image to your customers. If you plan a sawdust-on-the-floor kind of fish and seafood place, perhaps you'll want to hire college-age waiters and waitresses and dress them in jeans and T-shirts. If you have an English tearoom in mind, you may wish to hire middle-aged women to wait on your customers. When you plan the image you want to portray, however, be sure you're aware of the laws regarding age and sex discrimination, and don't break them.

Make out a list of the staff you'll need, on both a part-time and a full-time basis. Find out what salaries prevail in your town for those jobs, and figure that money into your initial budget. Remember that being skimpily staffed can cost you customers. If patrons have to wait too long for service or are served lukewarm meals because your waiters or chefs are overburdened, they won't return. So don't economize falsely.

Where you buy your food and other supplies can be an important element in the quality of your fare and, ultimately, in the profitability of your business. So shop for suppliers as well as supplies. Start by checking the yellow pages of your phone book for the listings under "Food Brokers." You may also find local publications for restauranteurs that will have an abundance of advertisements for food brokers. (One in the Minneapolis-St. Paul area, for example, is called *Food Scope*.) If you're buying an existing restaurant, like Lynn and Tom Wagstaff did, you will probably have access to the list of suppliers used by the previous owner.

For many restaurants, local grocery stores supply the perishables (particularly if the chefs don't need great quantities). Salt and spices, fresh vegetables and such may be nearly as cheap if you negotiate a deal with the local market as if you bought from a food wholesaler.

One small-restaurant owner got a full list of competent and comparably priced suppliers from a consultant with the Service Corps of Retired Executives (a free service of the Small Business Administration).

Compare price, quality and such elements as delivery when you choose your restaurant's suppliers. If one fish wholesaler, for example, has lower prices but does not provide delivery, it may be wiser for you to pay a higher price to a wholesaler who delivers.

You may need time to learn how much of each product to order. At first, try to order as little as possible. With time, you'll learn that your customers don't order broccoli or that shark sells better than tuna or that few of your customers order milk with their meals. Until then, chances are that you'll occasionally be stuck with broccoli that's going to seed, tuna that's no longer the "fresh catch of the day," or milk that's souring. With experience, over-ordering and consequent spoilage won't happen to you.

Make sure that you have plenty of storage space to hold your supplies, too. You'll likely find that it's more economical for you to buy many of your supplies frozen or canned instead of fresh—after all, they won't spoil as quickly. Having enough freezer space can also enable you to take advantage of discounts available for buying in quantity. But, of course, that means budgeting for an adequate freezer and pantry when you plan your restaurant.

Before you decide that all your food products should be canned, frozen or boxed to reduce spoilage, however, consider what kind of restaurant you really want to have and what prices you'll be charging your customers. Many seafood-lovers, for example, simply won't settle for frozen cod when they can get it fresh at the place down the street. And perhaps the gourmet touch of fresh, slightly under-cooked green beans with slivered almonds (instead of the rather anemic-looking ones that come from cans) on a plate might be just what makes your customers think, "What an elegant place!" On the other hand, if you're running essentially a low-cost fast-food operation, economizing may be your main priority. Just be certain that you've thought about what kind of food will satisfy the customers you have chosen to attract.

Your menu card is an important, and often expensive, element in your business, too. Many restaurants are now using chalkboards or oral menus, particularly if they frequently change the dishes they offer. Perhaps you might consider using either of these techniques, at least temporarily. Chances are you'll be changing your menu several times before you find one that works well for you.

Like the Wagstaffs, you may find that your original menu is underpriced and you're not making a profit. Scratched-out low prices replaced by higher ones may make your customers uneasy. Or your customers may order steak and avoid fish, making fish an unprofitable item for you to keep on hand. Trial and error is common at first, so try not to add unnecessary menu printings to your costs.

On opening day, be ready. Robert Patterson warns that word of a new restaurant spreads quickly and damningly. If your initial efforts are substandard, you may be out of business before you have the chance to reform. So, delay your opening for a few days, if necessary. Take a pointer from both the Barons and the Wagstaffs and invite your friends and relatives in before your restaurant officially opens. "Practice" on them until your menu is refined and your service is prompt and efficient. *Then* open to the public. The extra money spent by delaying those few days for your "dress rehearsal" can really save your show.

As opening day approaches, you'll need to let potential customers know you exist. Advertising is probably your best bet, and it's likely to be necessary at first. The Wagstaffs originally found that when they ran their first ad, customers were waiting in the parking lot for a table. Now, with an established clientele, they've cut back on their advertising budget. "We still maintain a listing in *Los Angeles* magazine, though," Lynn says. "That's really important in this town." If there is a corresponding publication read religiously by restaurant-goers in your town, consider spending some of your capital on ads placed there.

Do whatever you can to gain restaurant reviews, too. They can be a wonderful boost to your business. And learn what the important reviewers in your town look like so you can recognize them if they patronize your place. You will, of course, want to be sure they receive your top service.

Consider offering special promotions, too, perhaps a reduced-price menu for senior citizens, coupons offering two dinners for the price of one, a special grand opening celebration—anything that will bring your establishment to the attention of the public and get people excited about what you have to offer. After all, you have to become known to gain business.

And, if your restaurant's food, atmosphere, and service live up to expectations—both yours and your customers'—its reputation will spread and it will succeed.

Running a restaurant is, indeed, very difficult and risky work. It calls for far more than excellent cooking skills. You have to be a good host, a good businessman or businesswoman, and a good employee supervisor. In short, you have to be able to wear many other hats, in addition to your chef's hat.

Running a restaurant is one of the most difficult paths you can choose in the food business. But it's also one where you can actually become famous for your product. Like Charles and Jacqueline Baron, Lynn and Tom Wagstaff, you, too, have an opportunity to become both appreciated and admired by your customers—by running your very own, very special restaurant.

7

Uncommon Cooking Enterprises

One government publication lists 94 different food-and-beverage-related job categories. And another says that more than a million people are employed as cooks and chefs of one sort or another. Some of these jobs include those detailed in preceding chapters of this book: baking, catering, running a restaurant, opening a specialty foods store. But there are also many jobs that are less common and that can be done on a part-time basis, some of them actually created by the people who do them.

You may have an uncommon idea for a cooking business or job as well. Or you may wish to follow someone else's already proven idea. The jobs detailed in this chapter represent just a few of the unusual cooking-related jobs at which people make a living. Perhaps one will appeal to you . . . or maybe you'll invent your own.

FOOD STYLIST

Judy Prindle got her first job as a freelance food stylist when she was only 15. A food stylist is a person who cooks and arranges the foods used in still photographs and films.

"When I was 15, I was asked to bake a cake for an ad photograph and that's what I've been doing ever since," Judy says. She's now slightly over 30 and earning an excellent living preparing food for commercials shot in Los Angeles. She says that a food stylist job with a food manufacturer may require a degree in home economics, but that's not the case for people who do this work directly for photographers and production companies on a freelance basis. "I don't have a degree and my clients care only about whether or not I can cook and arrange the food attractively," she says.

Because Judy works mainly for motion-picture photographers, preparing the necessary food can mean a great deal of cooking. "You might need only one pretty cake for a still photograph, but you can use up 200 cakes for a commercial. Every time the actor cuts a slice, you need a new cake." And for one turkey commercial, Judy once roasted 150 of the birds in three days' time.

Food stylist is an occupation that doesn't require the capital investment of many other businesses. "I simply tell the production company how many ovens and what equipment I need and they rent everything for me," Judy says.

Her job does require more than good cooking skills, however. She needs to know how to arrange the colors and textures of foods attractively. She has to be able to work fast and to know how to make the food last under hot lights as well. "It's also very important that you use only the real products when you cook," Judy says. "People used to use shaving cream for whipped cream, things like that. You can't do that anymore because of the laws. I have to sign affidavits that I've actually used the advertiser's products."

Food stylist jobs are available in larger cities where commercials are produced, cookbooks are printed, and major food manufacturers are based. The pay you can expect to earn varies with the size of the city and with your experience. "Usually you're paid for a 10-hour day," Judy Prindle says. "That pay can range from about $50 to $300 a day in most cities." The top food stylists in the country, however, can earn as much as $1800 a day.

Because a job like Judy's is freelance, you won't work a 40-hour week. Judy says that most weeks she works three or four days a week, and that's considered a fairly full schedule.

If you're interested in becoming a food stylist, Judy suggests that you volunteer to help someone who's already established in that kind of work while you learn the job and make contacts for your own future employment.

FREELANCE DESSERT MAKER

Los Angeles caterer Marcia Matthews began in the food business as a freelance dessert maker. "I had a great recipe for carrot cake," she recalls, "and I was hired by a local bakery to bake it." Marcia's job was not only to bake the cakes, but to sell them as well. So she spent a portion of her time knocking on restaurant doors and talking to chefs. "One restaurant asked me to bake carrot cakes for them in their kitchen, so I did," she says.

That restaurant was Yellowfingers, a well-known eatery in the San Fernando Valley. Marcia's cakes were so well received by the restaurant's customers that they were written up in the *Los Angeles Times,* prompting a request for the recipe from *Gourmet* magazine.

Marcia also developed a very special recipe for chocolate mousse and sold that dessert to both Yellowfingers and the Sagebrush Cantina in Calabasas. "I did that kind of work for about three years," she says, "baking in the restaurant kitchens' off hours, usually early mornings, and Thursday and Sunday afternoons. I worked about 20 hours a week."

If you have a dessert specialty, working as a freelance dessert maker for a restaurant or two in your town can be a wonderful way to earn extra money. The restaurant benefits because it will likely pay a little less for your desserts than if they were purchased ready-made. And you will avoid the many legal entanglements inherent in setting up your own commercial kitchen elsewhere. The restaurant's kitchen is already approved by the health department and the other appropriate agencies, and you don't even have to pay the rent on it.

Marcia Matthews priced her carrot cakes and chocolate mousses "a little under my competition. I broke down my costs and added some profit. It wasn't a lot, but I did make some money."

If the idea of freelance dessert making appeals to you, prepare a few samples at home, figure out how much you'd have to charge for your specialty, and start knocking on restaurant doors, like Marcia did. Maybe, like she did, you'll find a whole new part-time career.

DEMONSTRATOR

Many good cooks make a part-time living demonstrating kitchen appliances and cooking gadgets. One of them is Marguerite Olds, who's been a demonstrator for Litton microwave ovens for about nine years.

"I'd always been interested in cooking," Marguerite says. "I even majored in home economics in college for awhile, but I quit college when I got married and never got my degree." Instead, she went to work as a secretary and later as a computer programmer, relegating cooking to the status of household activity and hobby.

When her two children were born, however, Marguerite stayed home to raise them until she felt the need to earn some money and get out of the house part-time. "A friend told me about a job demonstrating microwave ovens part-time on weekends and it sounded ideal for me," she recalls. "I applied and I got it." Much of her demonstration time was spent in department stores where the then-new ovens were being sold. Her job was essentially to help the store sell the ovens by making their use seem appealing and easy.

Many stores offered purchasers of the ovens a course in

how to use them and Marguerite was soon teaching those lessons as well. In addition, she trained other demonstrators as microwave oven sales increased. "Today, I teach one course a month for Litton in the San Fernando Valley and another in Thousand Oaks," she says. These classes are free for anyone who's interested. However, Marguerite points out that people are likely to find out about the Litton classes only through the company itself or through a department or appliance store that sells the ovens, so most students are recent or prospective purchasers.

Today, Marguerite Olds also gives lessons in microwave cooking at Everywoman's Village in Los Angeles. "My classes are all in microwave," she says, "but I try to make them different each time. For example, I've recently given classes in both basic microwave cooking and low-calorie microwave cooking." These courses generally meet one two-hour session a week for four or five weeks. "I cook one recipe of each food I'm demonstrating, usually enough to serve four to six people. I cook several different recipes at each session." So her students eat quite heartily during Marguerite's classes.

Marguerite is also often asked to give demonstrations for shops that sell microwave accessories and cookware. These shops advertise her appearances ahead of time and attempt to attract as many customers as possible.

If you're interested in becoming a demonstrator, your cooking ability and personality are more important than is your formal education. "You need to enjoy being with people," Marguerite says. "I had no public speaking or teaching experience, but I'm a ham to begin with." She thinks that a degree in home economics is unnecessary for most demonstrators, although "it would be needed if you wanted a full-time position supervising other demonstrators."

The money you can earn varies. Litton hires microwave oven demonstrators at $4.50 to $5.50 an hour to start and demonstrators are paid for five hours work when they demonstrate for four hours. The additional hour's pay is compensation for time spent shopping for food and planning the demonstration. The company also pays mileage and reimburses food costs. Marguerite Olds is now a consultant for Litton, so her earnings are higher.

The money she earns from microwave cooking courses not sponsored by Litton varies according to the price of the course and the number of students who enroll. "The courses cost around $25 for four classes," she says, "plus a lab fee that goes directly to me to pay for the food." About 40 percent of each student's fee goes to the instructor, and sometimes, if she demonstrates in a shop that sells microwave accessories, she also receives a percentage of the money brought in by merchandise sales.

Demonstrator jobs are available for a variety of food-related products and Marguerite Olds recommends that you not limit yourself to one kind of product. As more and more people buy a certain kind of cooking appliance or accessory, the market for it becomes saturated and the number of demonstrations given is reduced. For example, she says that demonstrations for microwave ovens were more numerous a few years back than they are now. So, look to other, newer kinds of kitchen products—food processors, for instance. Don't overlook, either, the fact that demonstrators are hired at food markets to cook and distribute samples of foods ranging from frozen hors d'oeuvres to cheeses to beverages.

If you have an outgoing personality and the idea of working at a variety of different locations appeals to you, consider becoming a part-time demonstrator. Contact the companies in your town that hire demonstrators directly or, if you live in a large city, you may be able to find an employment agency that specializes in demonstration jobs.

FOOD WRITER

Do you have an ability with the written word as well as a passion for cooking? If so, maybe your niche can be found in writing about food. One of the spin-off jobs that Marguerite Olds did for a time was writing a column on microwave cooking for the *Los Angeles Herald-Examiner*. And both Marlene Sorosky and Martha Stewart have written cookbooks in addition to running their teaching (and Martha's catering) businesses.

As with most other freelance jobs, your ability is more important than your academic credentials. If you want to write a cooking column for your local newspaper, for instance, write several installments on speculation, forming each around a specific theme and testing each recipe carefully. Add some interesting connecting information. (After all, newspapers can acquire a simple list of recipes free from food manufacturers, so they'll want something more from you.) Submit your package to the appropriate editor. What you can earn will be negotiable. Your best chance will be with small city newspapers, so your earnings may not be high at first. But once you're established, it's possible to syndicate your column, selling it to other small papers in different parts of the country.

If writing a cookbook is your dream, feel encouraged by the fact that more than 300 of them are published each year. Try to think of an unusual idea for yours. Betty Crocker, Fannie Farmer, and the like seem to have the market for general cookbooks covered. Maybe you'll want to write a cookbook about 100 ways to use yogurt; or about fantastic breads; or about simple, low-cost uses for tuna. Marlene Sorosky's book, *Cookery for Entertaining*, was about just that—marvelous menus for parties. And Martha Stewart's, also on entertaining, includes information on running successful parties, from sending out the invitations to cleaning up afterward.

Once you've refined your cookbook idea and assembled several of your carefully tested recipes, write a couple of chapters, add a detailed outline of the rest of the book, and begin submitting it to publishers. You can find publishers that buy cookbook manuscripts by looking in *Writer's Market* or *Literary Market Place* at your local library or by visiting a bookstore and noting the names of publishers who've done other books in your general category.

Still another kind of food writing is freelance magazine writing. Many magazines limit their food articles to those that are staff-written (you can check your favorite's policy in *Writer's Market,* too), but others buy from freelancers.

California State University, Northridge, journalism student Janice Henderson, for example, recently sold two foods articles to *Los Angeles* magazine. One was on chocolate desserts and the other on how to plan a delicious and sensuous evening around a Middle Eastern dinner. Both articles were humorously written and included several tested recipes. Janice also became involved in cooking for and setting up photographs of the foods she included in her articles.

If you want to submit your freelance food articles to magazines, there are two traditional ways to do it. The first is to write a "query letter" to the magazine's editor detailing your idea. Be sure that the letter represents your best writing, because it will serve as a sample of your ability at the typewriter. The second method is to write the entire article and submit it to the editor. In either case, be sure to enclose a stamped, self-addressed envelope to ensure that the editor will reply.

Still another way to write about food is to join the ranks of restaurant critics, many of whom are excellent cooks themselves. Your chances of being hired by a major publication are not good. After all, your competition includes such giants in the field as Gael Green, Mimi Sheraton, Lois Dwan, Patricia Unterman, Phyllis Richman, Robert Shoffner. But don't be too discouraged. There are still reviewing spots available on small publications, either your hometown newspaper (if you live in a small town), or emerging city and neighborhood publications. If becoming a restaurant critic interests you, try writing three or four sample critiques and submitting them to your selected publication.

FREELANCE BARTENDING

When people give a party, they often need help with

more than the food; they may well want bartenders, too. That was the idea behind Cheers, a small business started a few years back by two Long Beach State University students, Philippe Guiral and George Nagle.

Philippe and George had worked nights as bartenders in a hotel bar, work for which they'd had no special training. Philippe says that his sole preparation before applying for the hotel job was buying "one of those little *Mr. Boston* (drink recipe) books." With tips, the work paid fairly well, particularly for college students. Philippe, in the mid-1970s, was earning more than $50 a night.

As they became more proficient, customers began to ask Philippe and George to work at their private parties and the idea for Cheers was born. The two formed a partnership and each put $1000 into a bank account to cover the cost of advertising and business cards. Their first ads turned out to be a waste of money; three ads that cost $800 brought only two phone calls. But writing letters to local caterers was more productive. Philippe says that the caterers welcomed Cheers because it was a professional service and most had been plagued by bartenders who drank a large portion of what they poured.

Guiral and Nagle often purchase the liquor, beer, and wine for their parties and make suggestions to the hosts about the amount and varieties needed in addition to pouring drinks during the party itself.

After the second year, Cheers had grown to its present volume of business, about 35 jobs a year. The business is seasonal; holidays are very busy and January to summer relatively slow. The two students earn between $2000 and $3000 a year from Cheers for their part-time work.

If you enjoy tending bar and want to try it on a freelance basis like Philippe Guiral and George Nagle, your only investment need be in letters to local caterers, a uniform to wear during the parties, and such bar accessories as corkscrews and pour spouts. Cheers!

These are just a few of the dozens of ideas for uncommon

cooking jobs that you might consider. Many people, like some of these, have created their own uncommon cooking jobs. One New York woman, for example, works as a free-lance cook for people on the Pritikin diet for heart patients. Two Los Angeles women run Renta Yenta, a wide-ranging service business that offers, among other things, a catered breakfast-in-bed that's often given as a gift. A 9-year-old Montana farmboy bakes cookies and cupcakes after school and sells them to workers on an oil rig near his home. A California woman uses her cooking knowledge to work as a freelance kitchen planner. Sybil Henderson, mother of food stylist Judy Prindle, runs an advertising and public relations agency that specializes in food product accounts.

Give your imagination free reign. Even if you want only a part-time or freelance cooking career, there are literally hundreds of possible ways that you, too, can cash in on cooking.

8

Figuring Your Finances

Cliches become cliches, of course, because there is so much truth in them. The old saw, "It takes money to make money," is as true for food businesses as for any other kind. Since your purpose in having a cooking business is ultimately to make money with your cooking skills, you'll need cash to invest. Every cooking businesses requires some financial investment, although it can vary from the few bags of groceries that Holly Torath bought to teach her first cooking lesson, to the more than $100,000 Nadine Kalachnikoff invested to create Pasta, Inc.

In planning your own cooking business, it's important that you estimate carefully just how much money you'll need to start your business and to run it until it becomes well established and profitable. Don't be undercapitalized. That mistake is one of the leading causes of small business failure. When asked what they would have done differently, the answer given most often by cooking business owners interviewed for this book was, "I wish I had had more capital."

But how do you determine just how much capital you really need to give your business the kind of start it requires to prosper? There are several sources of excellent free and low-cost help that you can tap in planning your business. Perhaps the most complete and helpful source is the U.S. Small Business Administration. Use the appendix of this book to help find the SBA office nearest you, and call to request a copy of its publication, *Starting and Managing a Small Business of Your Own.*

The SBA office can also give you information on whether or not you qualify for an SBA loan, give you a schedule of the pre-business workshops it sponsors, help you develop a workable business plan, and arrange follow-up assistance. The SBA sponsors two organizations that offer help from people who've been successful in your business field: SCORE, the Service Corps of Retired Executives; and ACE, the Active Corps of Executives.

Tom Bronchetti, who a few years ago opened a tiny specialized restaurant in Santa Monica called The Chili Connection, says he and his partner got invaluable help from the SBA and SCORE. "We went to an all-day SBA lecture," he says, "and the speakers there told us what to expect when we opened our business. Then a couple of really good people from SCORE who'd once had restaurants in our area came by during our construction project and made suggestions. They were just great."

Take advantage of the help you can obtain from sources like the SBA. These knowledgeable people can help you plan your budget and find financing as well.

The major items for which you will have to allot funds are listed here. Sources like the SBA can aid you in deciding how much money each category is likely to require for your specific business in its particular location.

Rent and utilities. You will need a place to run your cooking business, whether you plan a catering service, or a full-fledged specialty food store. If you can operate out of your home, you'll probably cut your costs significantly, but that may not be legal where you live. And, even if you can run your business from your home, you're likely to need a second kitchen, like the one caterer Martha Stewart built in her Connecticut basement. If you cook professionally from your home, your utility bills will rise also. Figure these costs closely, and consider the cost of your lease as carefully as you consider your business location. The two are always intimately related.

Remodeling costs. Once you've found a site, it may well require remodeling to fit your own specifications. Your expenses here include materials, such as lumber, concrete, paint, plumbing, and shelving, as well as the labor to perform the remodeling job.

There are many ways to save money in remodeling, of course. Lynn and Tom Wagstaff, for instance, bought discounted fabric, and Lynn's mother sewed the curtains for Casa Monica. Charles and Jacqueline Baron made the tablecloths for Bonsoir Charles from bedsheets. Martha Stewart and Helen Benton bought used stoves, refrigerators, sinks, and cabinets for their catering kitchens. Be creative in planning your remodeling job. If you have a talent for construction or sewing, use it to cut costs. And don't feel that everything you buy has to be brand new.

License fees and deposits. Don't forget the cost of the licenses and permits you will need to start your business. These can range from a few dollars for a business license to many thousands for an alcoholic beverage license. Find out which licenses and permits are required, and budget for them. Remember, too, to include money for the deposits you may be required to make for such utilities as telephone, gas, and electricity.

Equipment. This category includes everything from baking pans to a delivery truck. Make a detailed list of everything you will need, even such items as potato peelers. Include here, too, the cost of items you will be likely to rent. Don't be persuaded that you have to own everything. Remember that Helen Benton feels her catering business was less profitable than it could have been because she gave in to the temptation to own all kinds of fancy serving pieces and chafing dishes. Today, she strongly recommends renting most of these items.

Insurance. If you're running a food business, having insurance is vitally important. If you don't have adequate coverage, a customer who becomes ill after eating your food (or even one who falls in the washroom of your restaurant) could bankrupt your enterprise with a lawsuit. Shop around for the best rates, but be sure that you're adequately covered. And, remember that unless you have incorporated your business, your personal assets could be attached in a judgment against your business. Saving on insurance can be false economy, indeed.

Maintenance. This category includes maintenance of your kitchen, its equipment, your delivery vehicles, and anything owned by your business. Maintenance can be a very difficult cost to estimate, but remember that needing a new motor for your freezer could eat up your profits for weeks. Or, if there aren't any profits yet, it could put you so far into the red that you won't be able to recover. The difficulty of estimating maintenance costs also points up another advantage of renting expensive equipment whenever possible. With rental or leasing, you know exactly what your monthly expenses will be, and maintenance is the responsibility of the rental company. They, not you, will have to bear the burden of the unknown.

Legal advice. You will need a good attorney to help you with the lease, the licenses and permits you are required to have, selection of the right insurance policy, and drawing up any partnership agreements or incorporation papers. Don't forget to include legal fees in your initial budget.

Financial advice. Just as you will need a good attorney, a good accountant will help plan your budget, prepare your tax returns, and give you advice on finding additional financing if it becomes necessary. Include financial consulting fees in your initial budget.

Taxes. Your accountant can advise you on how much money to budget for taxes. Be aware, too, that the legal form of ownership you select for your business (sole proprietorship, partnership, or corporation) will have an impact on your tax liabilities. Discuss this with your accountant and attorney before you make a decision.

Supplies. In a cooking business, the category of supplies includes not only the groceries you'll need to prepare your products, but such items as clean-up products and packaging as well. Packaging, particularly, can be quite expensive. Consider, for example, the round metal tins that keep cakes from the Miss Grace Lemon Cake Company fresh and undamaged during shipping. Each tin is placed inside a corregated box, and this double packaging is a significant part of each cake's cost.

With food, you must budget for spoilage. You cannot let your products sit for months until you need them, as you can with something like auto parts. Obviously, food will spoil.

Food business costs will fluctuate more than costs in most other businesses as a result of seasonal food prices. Holly Torath, for example, often visits three grocery stores for each party she caters, because food prices vary so widely. Not only will they vary from store to store, but seasonal foods can make or break your budget if you don't figure carefully.

Labor. Unless you plan a business that you can run all by yourself or with a partner, you'll soon have to hire help. And employees usually cost you more than the hourly wages you pay them. If you hire full-time employees, be prepared to add these extras to the cost of their wages: 6.13 percent for

Social Security payments; a variable percentage for worker's compensation (this depends upon the safety factor of the job and ranges from .45 to 51 percent); 3.6 percent or more for federal and state employment insurance; and any fringe benefits you offer, such as paid vacations, sick leave, health insurance, and life insurance. Because of these extra costs, try to hire freelance and temporary labor whenever you can. For example, if you run a catering service and you hire only freelance waiters, you can save significantly on your labor costs because you will not be liable for such extras as unemployment insurance.

Hire carefully. Your employees can make or break your business. Don't overhire or underhire, either. Hiring more employees than you need is wasteful, and hiring too few can make your enterprise seem slipshod and poorly managed, ultimately costing you valuable business.

And, if you plan to pay yourself a salary, include a reasonable figure for that labor expense, too.

Your living expenses during the break-in period. It's likely that you will take between three months and a year before your business begins to show a profit. Unless you have the luxury of another income to support your family during this time, you'll need money to live on. Though most financial counselors would probably disapprove, Lynn and Tom Wagstaff lived on their checking account overdraft fund during this period. Sandy Gooch's husband supported their family during the first two years of Mrs. Gooch's Natural Food Store. She reinvested all of her store's profits during that time, but now takes home a salary of about $20,000 a year. Nadine Kalachnikoff and her children lived on savings and child support payments while Pasta, Inc., got off the ground.

A safe amount to set aside during the first months of your new business is the salary you earned before changing careers. If you have not been employed previously, figure out your living expenses for a specific period of time (three months to a year), and then deduct the income you have from other sources to compute what additional amount you'll need.

Interest. Using other people's money, of course, costs you money. So remember to budget for the interest charges on your loans. At the present time, with the prime lending rate well into double digits, interest charges can be a very large percentage of your monthly budget.

Advertising and publicity. Potential customers need to know that your business exists, if you are to have a business at all. So put aside at least a little money for advertising and promotion. It needn't be a large amount, but it should be carefully spent. Loretta Shine of the Miss Grace Lemon Cake Company, for example, budgets for donations of her cakes to charity events. The cost is relatively low and the customers she gains with her free samples are well worth that cost. Sandy Gooch advises setting aside a more significant percentage of your projected gross income for advertising when your business debuts. She spent 10 percent of that figure on advertising when the Hermosa Beach branch of Mrs. Gooch's Natural Food Store opened, and her ads paid off by bringing thousands of people into her store.

Emergencies. This final category is also a most important one. What would happen, for instance, if your pizza oven suddenly refused to heat and you had to buy a new one immediately? Or, what if several of your credit customers were months late in paying you? What if an employee filed an expensive lawsuit against you, or if one of a thousand other possible emergencies occurred? The unexpected, too, must have a place in your budget or it can literally murder your business.

Prepare your first year's budget very carefully. Plan for every possible expense, and don't forget inflation. Use any help available to you to make sure your budget is as close as possible to what you'll actually experience. It's the surprises, the unplanned expenses, that will cause you difficulty.

In addition to help from the SBA or your local university's extension courses, strongly consider working for a time in a business similar to the one you want to own. This will give you hands-on experience and an opportunity to see what another company's balance sheet really looks like. It will allow you to talk with customers and find out what they like and dislike about the company. You can model your own business on their preferences. And finally, working in a similar company will give you the opportunity to see if you really like that kind of work. If it turns out to be disappointing, it's much less expensive to find this out as an employee than as a small business owner.

Providing that you now have a well-planned budget for your business, and that you know how much money you will need to start it and run it until it's in the black, the next question is where will you get the funds you need? There is a variety of sources you can pursue, and several are listed here:

Your savings. You may be one of the lucky ones who can finance your business totally from your savings accounts, or from the sale of stocks and bonds, or property you own. If you can do this, you will retain control over your business and save money as well, because you won't have to pay interest charges. Charles and Jacqueline Baron were able to finance Bonsoir Charles with approximately $50,000 of their own savings. And Helen and Bill Benton started The Thinnery bakeries with their savings of less than $10,000.

Most investors are reluctant to invest in a company if the owner doesn't have any of his own money on the line. So, even if you can't come up with all the money to cover your start-up costs, plan on investing some of your own cash.

Explore all your assets. You may have money you don't even know you have. For example, if you own a house, you may be sitting on a great deal of equity. You could sell it, take out a second mortgage on the house, or refinance the first mortgage. Nadine Kalachnikoff did that, raising $100,000 on her Georgetown home to finance Pasta, Inc. Consider, as well, such resources as cash value on your life insurance policies.

Money from relatives and friends. Many a small-business owner has started out by borrowing money from family and friends at favorable interest rates. Possibly you can do the same, for at least part of your initial investment. Lynn and Tom Wagstaff borrowed money from Lynn's parents to begin Casa Monica, and a year or so down the road, a good friend bought an interest in the restaurant, providing the Wagstaffs with enough cash to buy out their silent partner. Peggy Mathison invested about $65,000 of her own money in Custom Cookery, but five other women (her sister, a neighbor, and three old friends) invested lesser amounts and became minority stockholders. Money you acquire from family and friends can be treated in one of two ways: you can consider it a loan and repay it with interest; or you can sell them a portion of your business in return for their cash.

Bank Loans. Bank loans are difficult to arrange for new businesses. In general, banks will loan money only against your collateral, not against your equity. Professor Herbert Kierulff of the School of Business Administration at the University of Southern California, explains: "Financing your business is divided into two halves: the equity or risk portion, and the non-risk or collateralized portion. You can borrow money from a bank against a building, against equipment, against inventory. But you also need working (risk) capital, and that's what you have to get from your savings, common stock, or investors." Banks generally won't loan money to you except against collateral.

Remember, however, that you may arrange a bank loan against collateral you own that isn't a part of your business, such as your house or automobile.

Sometimes it's easier to obtain a bank loan by applying for one that's guaranteed by the Small Business Administration. The SBA guarantees up to 90 percent of the loan, so the bank takes less risk. The only firm SBA requirement for loan applicants is that they must have been turned down for a conventional bank loan at least twice, not a difficult criterion to meet today. However, because of the current tight money situation, many banks require that even for an SBA loan you must have been in business for two years and have a profitable track record. Check with your local banks for their requirements. Often small, independent banks are more receptive to small businesses than are larger ones. Generally, the interest rate you pay on an SBA loan is about 2½ percent above the prime lending rate. But it's renegotiated every four months and usually reamortized to keep the monthly payments constant, if interest rates are rising. The SBA also offers guaranteed loans at 13 percent interest for what it calls "socially and economically disadvantaged" borrowers. But as the national allotment for this program is only $500 million, it may be difficult to find money available.

If you have a good credit rating and are established with your bank, try to obtain a signature loan. This may not be enough to cover all your start-up costs, but such a loan may provide a portion of what you need to borrow.

Venture capitalists. Venture capitalists include individuals, investment companies, and groups who will invest in businesses in return for part ownership. Lynn and Tom Wagstaff found such an investor, a "silent partner," who contributed money but no management advice to help them start their restaurant. They later bought out the silent partner's interest in the business, giving him a small profit on his investment. You may be able to locate a venture capitalist for your business through friends, your attorney, or your banker.

Stock issue. If you decide to incorporate your business, your charter will specify the number of shares your corporation may issue. Selling some of these shares to others can raise cash in return for part ownership of your company.

If you have a truly workable idea for a cooking business, if you're willing to invest your own savings, and if you follow up on all possible routes for gaining additional financing (even in today's negative economic climate), you'll soon be in business for yourself. But it does take a sound financial plan and an unwillingness to take "no" for an answer.

9

The Legal Ingredients

Food businesses are subject to all the rules and regulations that any business faces, plus quite a few more that pertain only to companies selling food for public consumption. There are laws covering foods businesses on the federal, the state, and the local levels, beginning with the Federal Food, Drug, and Cosmetics Act.

To guide you through this maze of legal requirements, you'll need a good attorney, and it may be to your advantage to hire him or her on a retainer basis. He can be helpful to you when you're starting up your business, as well as during the time it's functioning (either smoothly or not-so-smoothly). In the beginning he will help you negotiate leases and contracts and assist you in finding out about and meeting the various rules and regulations that cover businesses like yours. Try to find an attorney who's experienced with businesses as much like yours as possible. For example, if you want to have your own restaurant, ask advice from

129

other restauranteurs in your community; hire an attorney recommended and used by them. Your family lawyer probably isn't your best choice here, even if he's been helping you with your personal legal work for years. You'll save money in the end by hiring a specialist because you won't have to pay for time he spends looking up your legal requirements; he'll already be familiar with them.

There are many, many categories of laws about which you'll need to know. The following list includes some, but not all, of them:

Business licenses and permits. Your foods business, like any other small business, will need to be registered and pay certain fees for the right to be in business. Your attorney should be familiar with the specific requirements in your town.

Zoning. Every town sets aside certain areas as residential, industrial, or for a variety of other special purposes. Where many home-based foods businesses get into trouble is with zoning regulations. If your neighborhood is zoned residential, chances are that you cannot legally operate your business there. Check zoning regulations before you sign a lease on a property you'd like to rent or buy.

Kitchen construction requirements. Using your family kitchen to cook foods for sale is illegal in most states. Health department requirements for commercial kitchens include specifications for floors, ceilings, ventilation, walls, and cleanliness. Make sure that the kitchen you want to use meets these requirements before you contract for it.

Labor laws. There are a potpourri of laws at the federal, state, and local levels that govern the employees you hire, ranging from the minimum wages you can pay them to affirmative action requirements to your various tax responsibilities. As pointed out previously, hiring an employee costs you much more than his or her hourly wage. And part of that cost is in the paperwork the government will require you to keep per employee.

Food and drug laws. A variety of federal requirements regulate the kinds of foods that can be sold for public consumption. For example, if you use saccharin in a food you prepare, you will have to meet certain requirements governing the amount that may be used in each product you produce and sell. Certain chemical additives, such as some food dyes and preservatives, are outlawed altogether.

Labeling requirements. Requirements for labeling food products change periodically and you must keep abreast of these changes. Avoid being caught with a large quantity of printed labels that no longer meet government requirements.

Truth in advertising laws. When you print your food labels, make up your menus, or run advertisements for your products, make sure you're being absolutely truthful. Even internationally famous restaurants, for example, have been publicly embarrassed with a fine when investigators discovered that their "Dover sole" was really taken from U.S. waters or their "whipped cream" was actually non-dairy topping.

Alcoholic beverage regulations. If you're running either a restaurant or a shop that will sell alcoholic beverages, you will find state and local laws that cover your operation. In some states, of course, it's illegal to serve alcohol at all. In others, patrons can bring along their own alcoholic beverages, but restaurants cannot sell them. In some areas, wine and beer licenses are relatively easy to obtain for only a small license fee, but a license to serve hard liquor costs considerably more money and is more difficult to come by. And in still other states, liquor licenses are limited in number and are sold for many thousands of dollars only when someone who has owned one dies or retires from business. Have your attorney check your state and community regulations carefully before you make a decision about whether or not to offer alcoholic beverages at your establishment.

These categories cover only a portion of the laws and regulations that will apply to your foods business. Others that pertain will be determined by both the kind of foods business you plan to have and the geographic area in which you'll be doing business. It would be nearly impossible for the typical small business owner to ferret out and comply with all of them on his own. Besides, you will want to spend your time doing more creative things in the kitchen. So don't try to economize by hiring an inexperienced lawyer or by trying to do without one at all. Get a good attorney who knows the foods industry and who can guide you competently through the legal maze of starting your own foods business.

Your attorney can also be of great help to you in making a vitally important decision: which legal form of business to choose for your enterprise. You have a choice of sole proprietorship, partnership, or corporation, and each form has advantages and disadvantages you'll want to consider.

Sole proprietorship. About 75 percent of all businesses in the United States are sole proprietorships. This is the simplest kind of business to set up, as well as the most common. To start your sole proprietorship all you have to do is get the appropriate business licenses, file a Certificate of Doing Business Under an Assumed Name (if you're using a business name), and begin.

A sole proprietorship is appropriate for you if you want to run your business alone, if you want to run it your way, and if you have enough money to finance it without taking in partners. A tax advantage of having a sole proprietorship is that you can write off your business losses against other income on which you have tax liability. For instance, you may have earned $15,000 by working at a salaried job for a portion of the year in which you started your business. If your business loses $5000 by the end of that year, you can reduce your $15,000 salary income by that $5000 before figuring your income tax. Or, if your spouse earns an income and you file a joint return, you can deduct your business loss from your joint income before figuring your tax. Of course, you hope that your business will not lose money for long, but a loss during at least part of your first year is probable.

The major disadvantage of the sole proprietorship is that your personal assets may be taken to pay off business liabilities. This becomes important if you are involved in a lawsuit or if your business fails and you cannot liquidate its assets for enough money to satisfy your creditors.

You should also be aware that, if you die, your sole proprietorship dies with you.

Partnership. A partnership can be the appropriate legal form of business for you if you need someone else's capital to help finance your business or someone else's expertise to help you run it.

There are two kinds of partnership agreements that you might set up. You are called a "general partner," and you can have one or more other general partners. General partners share equally in the financial and legal obligations of the partnership. Or, you might choose the other kind of partner, a "limited partner." A limited partner is a person who makes a financial investment in your business in return for a portion of it. The limited partner, however, does not share in the running of the business and is not personally liable for business debts as the general partners are. This latter form of business is not legal in all states, so check with your attorney.

A partnership might be an excellent choice for you if your skills are solely cooking skills and you need someone with good management abilities to help you. Choose your partner carefully, however. Many business experts say that you should choose a business partner with just as much care as you choose your spouse, and that makes good sense. You will have to share authority and responsibility with your general partner, so be sure that you're fully compatible. If things don't work out, after all, you're left with only a few options: you can buy out your partner, which you may not be able to afford; you can sell out to your partner, which means that you lose your business; or you can continue in an unhappy business relationship, which strips your business career of its enjoyability.

Like a sole proprietorship, a partnership leaves the general partners' assets open to confiscation to pay business debts. This is another good reason to be particularly careful in your choice of a partner. The actions of any one general partner, including the signing of contracts, can adversely affect the personal assets of the other general partners, even if they didn't approve or even know about the first general partner's actions.

If you decide on a partnership form of business, be sure to have your attorney draw up a partnership agreement. It should include the duties and responsibilities of all the partners, as well as specifications for one partner's buying out the other(s) if the liaison turns out badly or if a partner dies.

Corporation. A corporation may be the best legal form of business for you if you have considerable personal assets that you want protected in case your business fails. The law sees the corporation as a separate legal entity, in and of itself, unlike the way it regards the sole proprietorship and the partnership. A second advantage to the corporation is that it has an inherent permanence in the event that one of the principals dies. The owners of a corporation can also change easily through the sale of stock; in fact, the minor stockholders of many corporations often change on a daily basis.

To set up a corporation, you and two or more other persons must apply for a charter from the state in which you wish to operate your business. Requirements vary from state to state, but generally you will be required to file a Certificate of Incorporation, which details the names and addresses of the incorporators, the purpose and kind of business activity in which you plan to engage, the amount of stock you wish to authorize, and other details. Your attorney should help you file for incorporation and also prepare a pre-incorporation agreement between you and the other principals.

The major disadvantages of incorporating are financial. Because the law sees the corporation as a distinct entity, the business itself is taxed. If you serve as president and major stockholder, you will pay personal income taxes on both your salary and your share of the business' profits, and the corporation will pay taxes on those profits as well. This amounts to a form of double taxation. And, unfortunately, if your corporation loses money, you cannot deduct its losses from your other personal income before figuring your tax liability as you could under a sole proprietorship or a partnership. The corporation, too, is regulated much more closely by law than are either the sole proprietorship or the partnership.

Setting up a corporation also is not without its own expenses. This procedure can cost you from a few hundred to well over a thousand dollars.

With your attorney to help you choose your most logical legal form of business (sole proprietorship, partnership, or corporation), and to help make sure that you are in compliance with the myriad laws and regulations that apply, your business will be starting out on a proper foundation. You won't have to waste time worrying about legal complications or take a chance on your business being closed down because you have inadvertently violated a law. You can do just what you set out to do: run a business founded on your cooking skills.

10

Is the Food Business for You?

"When I opened my store, I changed psychologically," says Marlene Sorosky. "It made me into a businesswoman. It was not a hobby anymore." Marlene Sorosky's Cooking Center School and Shop is in the black now; it's a success. But it took much more than Marlene's cooking talents to make it so. She, like the other excellent cooks in this book, found that she drew upon many other talents, including some she didn't even know she had, when she started her cooking business. You will need those other talents, too, if your dream of a cooking business isn't to become a nightmare. Or else you will have to collaborate with others whose talents complement your own.

This list of questions was formulated from the advice given and the lessons learned by many people who've started their own cooking businesses. Your answers to them should help you decide whether or not a cooking business is really for you.

WHAT IS UNIQUE ABOUT YOUR IDEA FOR A COOKING BUSINESS?

Each and every person interviewed for this book stressed the importance of having a truly creative idea for your cooking business. It's assumed that your skills with food are superb or you wouldn't be considering starting a business based on them, but how are they *different?* Perhaps Loretta Shine of the Miss Grace Lemon Cake Company said it best in her advice to others thinking about starting a bakery: "Find your niche. What can you do better than anyone else? There are thousands of bakeries around all producing the same thing, but our cakes are unique. It's okay to charge higher prices. People will pay them to get something unusual and of good quality, something exciting."

That advice holds true, whether you want to start a bakery, a small restaurant, a catering service, a cooking school, a food store, a convenience foods business, or any other food-related enterprise. And being different doesn't have to mean being bizarre, either. Being different may simply mean that you're starting the first English tea shop in your town or the first catering service that can handle a fancy-dress ball.

ARE YOU TRULY COMMITTED TO YOUR IDEA FOR A COOKING BUSINESS?

Each person interviewed for this book also remarked about the hard work involved in starting a food business. As Marlene Sorosky says, a business is not a hobby. You can't have a half-baked commitment to it or you will fail.

Charles Baron of Bonsoir Charles advises planning your business on paper and then putting it aside for three or four months. At the end of that time, if the idea has paled for you (if you're not still excited about the prospect of your business), don't pursue it any further.

This question also implies a willingness to do *everything* involved in your business. Marlene Sorosky has done every type of work connected with her cooking school and gourmet shop. "I'm not ashamed to do the dishes here, to sweep out, whatever, to make my business work," she says. But she's found that others, among them groups of women to whom she's lectured at UCLA, are not willing to do that. "I'm shocked that they simply refuse to start at the bottom," she says. If you want to do *only* the cooking, perhaps you'd do better to keep your skills with food a hobby, not a business.

Be prepared, too, for the long hours that starting any small business requires. Having your own company does not mean working 9:00 a.m. to 5:00 p.m. in most cases. Sandy Gooch says she worked 14 hours a day, seven days a week, when Mrs. Gooch's Natural Food Store first opened. Loretta Shine and her family worked all night long during that first Christmas rush period at the Miss Grace Lemon Cake Company. Nadine Kalachnikoff has hired a live-in babysitter so that she can work well into the night when it's necessary at Pasta, Inc. Are you willing to work equally hard?

If not, and you still want to pursue a cooking business, consider doing it together with several other good cooks. Custom Cookery did that. Originally, Peggy Mathison says, the company was begun by six women, five of whom worked only part-time hours. When one's children were ill, someone else filled in for her. "We're really supportive of each other," Peggy said. With six to share the load, a less hectic schedule became possible. But the price these women paid was that no one of them had the potential for becoming wealthy on her part-time labor.

DO YOU HAVE A HEAD FOR BUSINESS?

Do you understand balance sheets? Tax forms? How to acquire financing or sell stock in your company? How to price your products so that they sell and you make a profit? Many good cooks do not. As Lynn Wagstaff of Casa Monica restaurant points out, "Many chefs are creative in the kitchen, but they don't really know what they're doing when it comes to running a business." Luckily, her husband, Tom, knows both cooking and business management.

A lack of business knowledge is one of the major reasons why some businesses started by excellent cooks don't make it. If you don't have these skills, however, that doesn't necessarily mean that you should forget about your dream. There are a couple of different things you can do to remedy this lack. One is to enroll in business courses and acquire those skills. Most major universities offer extension courses in starting and running a small business. Caterer and cooking teacher Holly Torath took one, a one-day seminar at UCLA. "It was wonderful," she says. "I've always had huge blocks about money. I was brought up to be somebody's wife, not to work. And I thought that handling and earning money was going to be somebody else's job. So going out into the hard, cruel world was a shock." As she listened to the two instructors of her extension course, however, she says, "I could see everything they were saying in terms of my own business. It was extremely helpful to me."

A second solution if you don't have a head for business is to find a partner who does, perhaps someone with no particular cooking skills. You can complement each other. Helen Benton found such a partner in her husband, Bill. When she ran Helen Benton Personalized Parties, later Carousel Catering, and still later The Thinnery bakeries, Helen enjoyed the luxury of worrying only about the food-related aspects of her businesses. Bill took over on finances and management, deciding everything from how to price their foods to remodeling their floor space. Each Benton is able to do what he or she does best and the result is a marvelously successful food business.

Sandy Gooch, too, realized that she knew little about business when she dreamed about opening Mrs. Gooch's Natural Food Store, so she hired Dan Vollard, who had experience as manager of another health food store, to manage hers. A short time later, Dan bought in and became a full partner with Sandy. Perhaps a similar situation will work for you. The important thing, however, is to recognize that certain business skills are necessary to the success of any small business. Without good management, the best idea in the world for cashing in on cooking won't work. And the best cook in the world will fail. So examine your skills, recognize your limitations, and do something about them.

DO YOU ENJOY MEETING PEOPLE?

No business can be run without contact with people. You will depend on customers, so it's vital that you, or someone in your business, meet people easily and well, and be able to sell your cooking services or products. Someone has to do the public contact for your company. Do you have the personality to do it yourself?

Peggy Mathison of Custom Cookery has a background in public relations. She spent many years meeting the public and the press for Marymount University, and now is an able spokeswoman for her own company. Martha Stewart was a successful stockbroker, a career that required her to entertain clients, sell stocks, meet and greet new people. Today, she's using those same skills to build her catering business. Holly Torath was a schoolteacher, so she was used to standing in front of a class and speaking. She uses those same abilities today to teach cooking and in catering.

Do you have similar abilities? They don't have to have been honed at a paid job. Perhaps you love to give large parties and are successful at it. Maybe you've been active in your church or temple and are used to addressing the congregation. Possibly you've been in charge of recruiting volunteers for your local hospital. If you meet new people easily and are usually able to persuade them to do or buy something, you probably have the right kind of personality to sell your company and its products or services to the public. If not, if the idea of meeting people and convincing them to part with their money in exchange for your cooking scares you, find someone else to help with that part of your business. Stay in the kitchen and leave the public contact work to a partner or employee.

ARE YOU COMFORTABLE WITH RISK-TAKING?

Starting your own business involves taking both financial and personal risks, even if your own cooking-related business idea is merely writing a cookbook in the privacy of your home. (You could be using your writing and recipe-testing time earning money elsewhere, and another, less risky job would place your ego in less jeopardy, too.)

Knowing that you're responsible for other people's money and perhaps the financial survival of your family as well can be ulcer-producing. Some people simply cannot take that kind of pressure. Can you? Marlene Sorosky, for example, admits that she went into psychotherapy before she could work up the nerve to start her cooking school and gourmet shop. As a housewife who made an income teaching cooking in her home, she was used to taking very few risks. But, as an entrepreneur, she was called upon to take great risks: signing a store lease; commiting herself to a remodeling plan; borrowing $90,000 from a bank; hiring a staff who would depend on her for their livelihoods; purchasing merchandise and hoping it would sell. "I was petrified," she says. But, with help, she was able to take the risk of starting her new business and seeing it through. After a year of grueling work, along with delight in seeing her risks begin to pay off, Marlene was finally able to relax a bit and enjoy her business. Could you withstand an equal ordeal?

And what if your business fails? Could you withstand that ordeal? The chances that your new business will succeed don't look very good on paper. Professor Herbert Kierulff of the School of Business Administration at the University of Southern California points out that about half of all new businesses fail within the first year and 80 percent fail within five years. Of course, the way those statistics are gathered often makes your chances look blacker than they really are, but there's no doubt that starting a new business of any kind, whether it's a bakery or an auto repair shop, is risky. And, if you're likely to fall apart under the stresses inherent in taking that large a risk, your business is already on the road to failure. Ironically, you have to be able to accept the possibility of failure before you can succeed.

IS YOUR FAMILY SUPPORTIVE OF YOUR VENTURE?

Professor Kierulff says that it's vital that your spouse be 100 percent in favor of your venture into business. "You'll come home with all kinds of anguish at first," he says, "and lack of support from somebody dear to you can be devastating. The divorce rate can be pretty high under those circumstances."

Sandy Gooch can attest to that. She acknowledges that her marriage had problems to begin with, but she also feels that the pressures of starting, and succeeding in, her new foods business made those problems worsen until she and her husband finally divorced.

But having your own business can also be very good for your marriage, particularly if your family is involved in it. Professor Kierulff says that a family business can help make a solid family. "In a family business, everyone works together and they all have their own responsibilities. Everyone feels needed. That's much better than the small business where the entrepreneur is taken away from his family, causing rifts."

There are advantages for your children if you have your own food business, too. "It's a kind of business children can relate to," says Sandy Gooch. "Children like food." And it's often the kind of business in which they can work alongside mom and dad, too. Loretta Shine has employed her four children at various times in the history of the Miss Grace Lemon Cake Company. "When my children are working for me, they can't argue like they might at home," she says. "I'm harder on them than I am on my other employees. I expect them to set an example. I've threatened to fire them once or twice, but I've never had to.

"It's been nice that my children could work with me," Loretta continues. "They've gained a different view of me and I think more respect for me, too. I'm hard on them, but they know they've always got a job here if they need one."

Marlene Sorosky has employed her two older daughters on occasion, too. "My kids wrap, stock, store, deliver, everything. I pay them just like I would any other employee."

And Peggy Mathison says that many of the 23 children of

Custom Cookery's staff have worked there. "My daughter is our lawyer and some of the younger ones have worked clearing out the parking lot, painting the store, cleaning up, just about anything that needs to be done. We pay them all."

Having your own cooking business can tighten family bonds. Or it can actually sever them. It all depends on how much your family believes in, and participates in, your cooking business.

CAN YOU KEEP FROM OVEREATING IF YOU'RE AROUND FOOD ALL DAY?

This question may sound unimportant at first, but it's really not. Loretta Shine says that one of the most difficult things about running the Miss Grace Lemon Cake Company is being near food all day every day and not being able to snack constantly "without becoming a tub." She keeps her figure trim, but not without exercising a strong will power. "I find I don't want to cook as much at home anymore," she says, "but I admit I never get tired of eating. It's a horrible fight."

Some lose that fight, at least occasionally. *New York Times* restaurant critic Mimi Sheraton had to take a five-month leave of absence from her job in 1980, for instance, because her 5-foot 5-inch body had ballooned to 197 pounds. She lost 37 pounds during her time off, but still had 20 more to lose when she resumed her schedule of nightly restaurant visits.

Most people find they feel better about themselves when they look trim, and feeling good about yourself is an important element in your being successful in business. So ask yourself whether or not you can stand to be around food constantly without turning into an overweight, and unhappy, glutton.

Are your answers to all of these questions satisfactory? If so, and if you can acquire adequate financing for your project, chances are good that your idea for cashing in on cooking will succeed. Becoming a successful food entrepreneur requires a unique idea; a certain kind of personality; a strong personal support system; and, of course, excellent cooking skills. If you have all of these things, you, like the men and women in this book, are very likely to make it big cooking for cash.

11

Cash In!

Creating and working in your own special career in cooking not only enables you to earn an income, it allows you to do work you like doing as well. Over and over again the people profiled in this book talked about loving their work. Charles Baron mentioned his excitement at watching the pleasure of his restaurant guests when they ate a meal he had prepared. Helen Benton felt a thrill when overweight or diabetic people with a love of sweets told her they thought The Thinnery was a gift from heaven. Sandy Gooch was delighted whenever she was able to convince school-children that healthy eating was not only good for their bodies but tasty, too. Holly Torath spoke of feeling extreme pleasure and a strong sense of accomplishment when a bride and groom raved about the wedding cake she'd created for their special day.

As these people have related here, starting your own cooking business is not easy. You have to have the right idea, enough financing and the correct combination of skills and people to make it work. It's much safer to remain a housewife, or an accountant, or an elementary school-teacher, or a salesman. But it may not be nearly as gratifying for you if what you really love to do is cook.

Being a good cook is a very special skill. It took cooking teacher Marlene Sorosky some time to realize that. "I used to think that anyone could cook," she says, "but now I realize that it's a creative sense. It's a precious gift that you can choose to keep for your private use or to turn into profit and personal satisfaction in the outside world."

Conquering the business world with that gift can bring you a great sense of accomplishment. "I feel better about everything now," says Marlene Sorosky. "Before (when I was a housewife), I felt like half a person."

Nadine Kalachnikoff, too, feels much better about herself since she's made a success of Pasta, Inc. "Having the store has changed all my values," she says. "I used to think that I had to have a man to support me, but now I know that I don't." She adds, "Being independent has changed my thinking and now I know that I can have a relationship with a man if I want to, but it's not necessary for my survival or the survival of my sons."

Tom Wagstaff and his wife, Lynn, visibly enjoy the sense of celebrity that running Casa Monica brings them. Both cite feeling and being treated "like movie stars" by their customers. They enjoy having accomplished something that many others dream about, but don't have the courage (or perhaps the skill) to do.

Whether or not a career in cooking is right for you is, of course, your own decision, and one you'll need to share with your family. As the people in this book have shown, there are numerous possible choices, from those requiring only a few hours a week of your time to ones that could grow into a nationwide chain under your supervision. There are all levels of financial investment possible, too, depending upon what you choose to do.

You already have at least half of what it takes, that creative sense inherent in being a good cook. If you have, or can acquire, those other necessary ingredients—financial backing; personal support, the ability to take risks; a unique idea; a good business sense; the personality of an entrepreneur; you, too, can create your own unique recipe for cashing in on cooking.

Good luck. And bon appetit!

Appendix

The following listings can be of help to you in planning and implementing your own cooking business. They can also be of help in leading you to other sources of information.

GOVERNMENT AGENCIES

U.S. Small Business Administration
1441 L Street NW
Washington, DC 20416
202-653-6365
Regional Offices:
  Region I
  60 Batterymarch
  Boston, Massachusetts 02110
  617-223-3224

  Region II
  26 Federal Plaza
  New York, New York, 10007
  212-464-0100

  Region III
  1 Bala Cynwyd Plaza
  Bala Cynwyd, Pennsylvania 19004
  215-597-3311

151

Region IV
1401 Peachtree Street
Atlanta, Georgia 30309
404-257-0111

Region V
219 South Dearborn Street
Chicago, Illinois 60604
312-353-4401

Region VI
1720 Regal Row
Dallas, Texas 75235
214-749-1011

Region VII
911 Walnut Street
Kansas City, Missouri 64106
316-758-1212

Region VIII
1405 Curtis Street
Denver, Colorado 80202
303-327-0111

Region IX
450 Golden Gate Avenue
San Francisco, California 94102
415-556-9000

Region X
710 Second Avenue
Seattle, Washington 98104
206-442-5676

U.S. Department of Health and Human Services
Food & Drug Administration
5600 Fishers Lane
Rockville, Maryland 20852
301-443-3380

Check your local telephone directory for state and community health departments as well.

PROFESSIONAL AND TRADE ASSOCIATIONS

American Bakers Association
2020 K St. NW
Washington, DC 20006
202-296-5800

American Dairy Association
6300 N. River Road
Rosemont, Illinois 60018
312-696-1860

American Meat Institute
P.O. Box 3556
Arlington, Virginia 22209
703-841-1030

Associated Retail Bakers of America
6525 Belcrest Road
Hyattsville, Maryland 20782
301-277-0990

Association for Food Service Management
4902 Tollview Drive
Rolling Meadows, Illinois 60008
312-398-3140

Distilled Spirits Council of the US, Inc.
1300 Pennsylvania Building
Washington, DC 20004
202-628-3544

Food Marketing Institute
1750 K Street NW
Washington, DC 20006
202-452-8444

Grocery Manufacturers of America, Inc.
1425 K Street NW
Washington, DC 20005
202-638-6100

International Chefs Association
121 West 45th Street
New York, New York 10036
212-256-7625

International Frozen Food Association
919 18th Street NW
Washington, DC 20006
202-296-4080

Les Amis Du Vin
2302 Perkins Place
Silver Spring, Maryland 20910
301-588-0980

National Alcoholic Beverage Control Association
5454 Wisconsin Avenue NW, Suite 1700
Bethesda, Maryland 20015
301-654-3366

National Association of Convenience Stores
5205 Leesburg Pike
Falls Church, Virginia 22041
703-671-0054

National Association of Retail Grocers of the US
Sunrise Valley Drive
Reston, Virginia 22090
703-860-3300

National Food Brokers Association
1916 M Street NW
Washington, DC 20036
202-331-9120

National Frozen Foods
Box 398
Hershey, Pennsylvania 17033
717-534-1601

National Licensed Beverage Association
1025 Vermont Avenue, Suite 601
Washington, DC 20005
202-737-9118

National Milk Products Federation
30 F Street NW
Washington, DC 20001
202-393-8151

National Restaurant Association
1 IBM Plaza, Suite 2600
Chicago, Illinois 60611
312-787-2525

Quality Bakers of America Cooperative
1515 Broadway
New York, New York 10036
212-790-9200

Tea Council of the USA
230 Park Avenue
New York, New York 10017
212-986-6998

United Fresh Fruit and Vegetable Association
1019 19th Street NW
Washington, DC 20036
202-293-9210

Wine Institute
165 Post Street
San Francisco, California 94108
415-986-0878

Index